100 IDEAS
FOR TEACHING SCIENCE

CONTINUUM ONE HUNDREDS SERIES

OTHER SCIENCE TITLES

100 IDEAS
FOR TEACHING
SCIENCE

Sharon Archer

continuum
LONDON • NEW YORK

This book is dedicated to my parents and my husband for their
unwavering support and to the Science staff at Copleston High School
for allowing me to become the teacher I currently am.

Continuum International Publishing Group

The Tower Building   80 Maiden Lane
11 York Road   Suite 704, New York
London   NY 10038
SE1 7NX

www.continuumbooks.com

© Sharon Archer 2006

First published 2006
Reprinted 2007, 2008

British Library Cataloguing-in-Publication Data
A catalogue record for this book is available from the British
Library.

ISBN: 978–0–8264–8547–2 (paperback)

Library of Congress Cataloging-in-Publication Data
A catalog record for this book is available from the Library of
Congress.

Designed and Typeset by Ben Cracknell Studios
Printed and bound in Great Britain by MPG Books Ltd,
Bodmin, Cornwall

CONTENTS

SECTION 4 Dealing with a practical

SECTION 5 Fun class activities

SECTION 6 Just biology

SECTION 11 Some fun homework activities

SECTION 12 Revision techniques

SECTION 13 Using ICT

SECTION 14 **Reducing the marking load**

SECTION 15 **Science in the outside world**

SECTION 16 **Maintaining the WOW factor**

This book contains 100 great ideas to help science teachers provide stimulating and meaningful learning experiences for their students. This list of ideas is not extensive and I am sure you will be able to think of many more thought-provoking ideas once you have tried some of these.

Section 1 starts by looking at some of the general strategies I have used to help provide my students with a safe and stimulating learning environment, as well as some advice on preparing, and using, some inspiring and exciting resources for your students.

It is firmly believed that every lesson (or set of lessons) should begin with a starter activity and end with a plenary session. This could be as simple as some quick-fired questions to access prior knowledge, or summarize the information learnt in the lesson, or as complicated as the production of a summary of the whole unit of work. In Section 2 you will find some interesting science starter activities, while Section 10 discusses some of the summary work that my students and I have carried out.

In Section 3 you will find a couple of ideas to help you and your students have effective discussions, which will not only help enhance their scientific knowledge and understanding, but also boost the confidence of your quieter students.

One of the most challenging aspects of teaching science, when compared to some other subjects, is dealing with a practical situation. Section 4 gives several ideas on how to make this aspect of your teaching less stressful, including a number of ways of organizing your students at the beginning of these sessions. In addition, some of these ideas will help you, with the help of your students, to ensure that the equipment is returned to the prep. room ready to go out to the next class. This is not only good practice, but will also help you maintain a good working relationship with your science technicians.

Section 5 contains three simple experiments that your students will really enjoy. A real opportunity to remind them that science is fun.

The next three sections in this book, Sections 6, 7 and 8, discuss some exciting activities related to biology, chemistry and physics. You will however be able to adapt these ideas for use with other topics, and some alternatives have been highlighted in these sections, so please have a look at them all and adapt as necessary to the topics you are teaching.

When I started teaching, one of the things that came as the biggest shock to me was how many pupils did not know how to complete a scientific investigation, including 'simple' things like plotting a graph with an appropriate scale or deciding on the apparatus to use to measure 50 cm³ of water. It soon became obvious to me that it is very important that we teach our pupils investigation skills – they do not just happen and they need constant practice. Section 9 looks at some of the ideas I find helpful when teaching these skills.

Homework is always a bone of contention, with some students, and I feel it is important to provide exciting homework activities, as well as stimulating classroom experiences. Section 11 discusses a few ideas which are suitable homework activities to enhance the students' learning, while also being enjoyable tasks to complete.

Revision is an essential prologue to tests and examinations but the students always find this challenging and often feel it is unnecessary. I find these sessions easier if I use a variety of different techniques to help the students. This not only helps alleviate the boredom factor, but also allows the students to find a method that suits their particular learning style. It is important to remember that students need to be taught how to revise, it rarely comes naturally. You will find some advice on revision techniques in Section 12.

Over the last ten years technology has advanced at an alarming rate and our students tend to know more about computers that we do. I feel that it is essential for us to use ICT whenever, and wherever, possible to provide our students with effective learning opportunities, not just because it is there. Section 13 discusses a few ICT related activities I have used with my students, although I am certain there are many more activities you could think of after trying out a few of these ideas. In addition, there are a couple of suggestions on dealing with access to computers, which can be an issue at times. Remember, students love working on the computer and will sometimes find the information 'more interesting' than using a book. I'm not quite sure what the psychology is on this, but maybe it is related to the fantastic colours and the interactive nature of some of the computer programs.

One of the most stressful aspects of teaching any subject, in my opinion, is keeping up with all the marking (especially as I tend to be one of those less than realistic teachers who tries to mark everything fully). Section 14 discusses some of the strategies I have used to help lower my marking load over the years, while still providing my students with essential feedback on their work.

Science happens all around us every day, but pupils sometimes find it difficult to relate this to their science lessons. Section 15 presents a couple of ideas to help bring this to the forefront of the students' minds, while also allowing you opportunities to discuss current events with your students.

And finally, Section 16 includes some of the experiments that have impressed my students in the years I have been teaching science. These demonstrations have helped them see why science is such a fascinating subject as well as stimulating their need to know more about their surroundings and how things work. I hope you and your students enjoy them as much as we have.

I hope the ideas in this book inspire you, but the best advice I can give you is:

> Always remember the reasons you are enthralled
> by science and why you chose to teach science.

Teach with enthusiasm and you are guaranteed to inspire your students – a teacher's ultimate goal after all!!

Sharon Archer

General ideas

IDEA 1

PROVIDING A STIMULATING ENVIRONMENT

It is firmly believe that people are more productive if they are surrounded by an organized and friendly working environment. I firmly believe that this is particularly true of children and, as teachers, we need to ensure that we provide an environment in our classrooms that is conducive to good working practices.

There are several things that I recommend to help turn your classroom into an organized and friendly working environment to allow your students to feel secure and happy in their work:

○ have specific areas for different equipment, e.g. books, paper, colouring pencils, glue, scissors, glassware;
○ make sure all pupil equipment is clearly labelled, e.g. lined paper, graph paper, beakers (colourful labels work best to liven up the environment);
○ include colour wherever you can (e.g. cover display boards in bright colours);
○ display examples of students' work (an excellent motivation factor);
○ display appropriate keywords for all teaching units (make sure pupils know where these are);
○ make sure working areas are kept clear and clean;
○ display posters of key scientific facts;
○ display posters of upcoming events, e.g. science week;
○ provide space for pupils' belongings and make it clear where they are to put things, e.g. coat hooks, space for bags.

It is also important to change your room displays on a regular basis or they simply become wallpaper for the students.

The best ways of ensuring good behaviour in your classrooms (and therefore maximum learning opportunities) is making your students feel welcome and valued. One of the most effective ways of doing this is making sure you praise students at every opportunity.

There are several ways of doing this, including:

o give verbal praise during or after good work is completed (works well in front of the whole class);
o write praise in pupils' books;
o include stamps and stickers in pupils' books;
o issuing credit (or merits) in line with your school policy;
o send letters home commenting on exceptional work (remembering that some 'less than perfect' work may be the best a particular student is capable of;
o give small prizes for specific pieces of work.

These ideas even work for the older students (my sixth form will freely admit to being open to bribery if chocolate or sweets are on offer and they get very excited if they receive stickers on their work).

MOTIVATING YOUR STUDENTS

Preparing resources for my classes is one of the most enjoyable aspects of my job, although it is also one of the most time consuming. Listed below are a couple of ideas to help reduce the workload involved, while still allowing you to provide your students with stimulating activities.

PRODUCING RESOURCES AS A DEPARTMENT

This is something my department is very good at doing. Whenever a scheme of work is written, or reviewed, the required resources are provided for two or three class sets. These resources are then kept by the laboratory technicians and are supplied for the required activity. This is still time consuming but results in the workload being spread across the whole department and it tends to be carried out at the quieter times of the year, e.g. during the latter part of the summer term.

USING ADMINISTRATION OR TECHNICIAN TIME

Some schools have 'administration time' or 'technician time' for their teaching staff. This can be used in a variety of ways including the following:

USE OF ADMINISTRATIVE TIME

If you are 'not very good' on the computer then you could draw out a rough copy of what you want your worksheet, or other resource, to look like and then pass it on to the administrative staff to type it up for you (they tend to have better skills in this area than I have). You could also ask them to print out the required number of copies of the resource to save you time here as well.

USE OF LABORATORY TECHNICIAN TIME

I have often asked my laboratory technicians to photocopy examination papers or laminate worksheets and card sorts as this can also be very time consuming.

The important point with any of these ideas is to be organized and prepare resources in advance so that you can enlist the help of others. You must also make sure your requirements are very clear to avoid disappointment.

Card sort activities are an effective way of checking pupils' knowledge of a particular topic. I have found that producing relevant statements on card and laminating them makes these more hardwearing and so reusable without them looking tatty and unimportant.

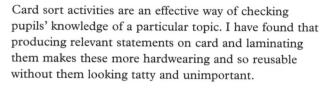

GENERAL INSTRUCTIONS

○ Write true and false statements (use Microsoft Word or you could hand write them if you prefer).
○ Print out (or photocopy) eight copies of these statements.
○ Cut out the individual statements.
○ Cut up card to the required size (A7 or A8 works well).
○ Stick the statements onto cards (I use a different colour of card for each set).
○ Laminate cards (ensuring you have a reasonable gap between each card).
○ Cut up laminated copies.

The first time I produced a class set of true and false statements I was shocked by the amount of time it took, although they were hardwearing and have been used several times and still look good. Listed below are some of the ideas I have since discovered to help alleviate some of the time issues:

○ keep number of statements to a minimum;
○ print statements in boxes to make it easier to cut them out;
○ use a trimmer to cut out statements (and cards);
○ print statements onto stickers then simply 'stick' onto card;
○ print statements straight onto card – difficult if you are using dark card;
○ laminate statements on coloured paper instead of card;
○ stick the statements onto A4 card then laminate and cut up.

PRODUCING CARD SORT ACTIVITIES

My recommendation is to try some of these ideas and decide which you personally prefer. Opinions on this within my department vary, although I prefer the use of stickers, stuck onto A8 card followed by lamination.

See Idea 10 for some examples on how to use card sort activities.

Worksheets are a very important resource in the science laboratory. They are one of the best ways of providing students with detailed instructions for the experiment they are investigating. They can however also be used for other activities, including sets of questions to consolidate knowledge of a particular topic, and providing information to research a scientific idea.

There are several ways of obtaining worksheets for your classes including:

PHOTOCOPYING WORKSHEETS

There are many companies that provide scientific worksheets which are copyright free; there are even some available on the Internet. This is definitely the least time consuming option but does not always give you exactly what you require and can result in poor quality worksheets if the original is not available when more are required.

PRODUCING YOUR OWN WORKSHEETS

This is definitely the best option in my opinion. It allows you to design the worksheet to your exact requirements and also allows you to differentiate the worksheets for your gifted and talented individuals as well as your special needs children. I tend to use Microsoft Word to do this as it allows me to include appropriate images (scanned images and clip-art work well) as well as the required text. Having produced the worksheets it is also very easy to print more as required.

SHARING WORKSHEETS

I always share my own worksheets with other members of my department as I do not see the point of 'repeating the work'. This also results in other members of my department sharing their work with me, always a good thing!

When I started teaching I found that some of the worksheets available were difficult to read (mainly due to their being photocopied several times) and quite frankly uninspiring.

The following ideas are some that I have used since to provide my students with some more professional-looking worksheets. Students of all age ranges have responded well to these ideas and I believe that this has had a knock on effect on their ability to recall information related to particular topics.

o Use a font which is easy to read (I prefer 'Comic Sans').

o Make sure the font size is easy to read (11 or 12 point works well).

o Make sure you spread out the text and break it up with diagrams to make the worksheet more readable.

o Include relevant clip-art images to add a hint of humour to the worksheet (e.g. a clip-art of a smiling atom at the top of a worksheet on atomic structure tends to make the pupils smile also).

o Include relevant clip-art images to add some colour to your worksheet.

o Print worksheets in colour on white or cream paper.

o If coloured printers are unavailable, or too expensive, then print worksheets on coloured paper.

o Laminate instruction worksheets (mounting on card before laminating also helps make them look more important).

In addition, if students are to stick worksheets into their books make sure they are trimmed to fit the page and give them time in the lesson to stick them in. This prevents the 'dog-eared' look often seen where worksheets are sticking out all over the place, or falling out of their books – does this really inspire pride in their work?

Displaying pupils' work is a great motivation factor for your students. I am always surprised at how important this is to students of all age ranges. They take great pride in having their work displayed and it also shows them that you value their work.

I feel that it is important to display as many pieces of student work as you can. Listed below are some of the ideas I have used over the years:

o cover display boards with brightly coloured paper;
o add attractive borders to your display boards;
o mount pupils' work on coloured card or paper before displaying;
o mount work individually or in sets;
o arrange the work in a pattern, rather than just in straight lines;
o encourage pupils to take pride in their work and include their names;
o laminate pupils' work if displayed in open areas to prevent damage from passing students etc.;
o use window space as well as wall space (be careful not to block out too much light);
o make sure you return pupils' work to them when you change the display;
o change displays regularly to prevent them becoming wallpaper.

Putting up displays can be time consuming, a real issue for a busy teacher, but the dividend this pays in terms of the relationships formed with your students makes it well worthwhile. It is important to realize that you do not need to put up a display all in one go, the pupils actually enjoy watching 'a work in progress'. You could also ask the students to help you put up their display, an additional motivation factor. Some students really love this and I have actually seen some students painting the display board with relevant images before displaying their work. Another way is to ask support staff to put up the actual display, but remember to let them know exactly what you expect to avoid disappointment.

DEALING WITH GRAFFITI

GRAFFITI ON DESKS

It is inevitable that some graffiti will be found on classroom desks, especially wooden science desks, even if it is simply a tribute to the latest 'pop group'.

I firmly believe that it is important to remove any graffiti as soon as possible (ethanol and cotton wool works well for this). This not only sends a powerful message that you will not tolerate this (and other inappropriate behaviour), but also prevents an excessive amount of graffiti appearing seemingly overnight if the original graffiti is not removed. It is also unfair to expect other pupils to sit at desks covered in graffiti, this does not put forward a positive working environment.

I also make it very clear to my students that if they are caught vandalizing my desks then they will spend time cleaning all of them – an excellent deterrent for any would-be desk artists.

GRAFFITI ON BOOKS

Again it is inevitable that some graffiti will be seen on pupils' books (most people are guilty of 'doodling'). However, this must be dealt with promptly to ensure pupils are aware of your high expectations regarding the looking after of their books.

My suggestion on this is very simple. Tell the student to cover their book by the next lesson, or you will provide them with some attractive 'flowery' wallpaper to do this with. You will be surprised how quickly most books will be covered given this choice. Even if you do have to provide them with some wallpaper, the actual problem will still have been solved with the minimum of fuss. I usually buy a cheap roll of wallpaper during the sales from my local DIY store in anticipation of this.

Starter activities

IDEA
9

An excellent starter activity for all year groups that involves little preparation but maximum learning. Not only does it help students learn how to spell some of the longer, more difficult scientific terms, but it is also fun.

Anagrams simply involve giving the students a scientific term related to the lesson being taught. Pupils are then asked to write down as many words, of three or more letters, as they can from this word. To encourage individual work I often run this as a competition to see who can get:

○ the most words;
○ the longest word.

GENERAL RULES
1 No plurals.
2 No names.
3 No slang words.
4 Can only use each letter once in any individual word (unless the letter appears twice in the original word).

Some of the words I have used include:

○ Polymerization (when discussing polymers and plastics);
○ Phenolphthalein (when discussing indicators);
○ Sedimentation (when discussing rock cycle);
○ Photosynthesis (self explanatory really!);
○ Chromosphere (when discussing formation of elements).

This activity allows you to access pupils' prior knowledge of a subject before building upon this knowledge, and is therefore suitable for a variety of age groups and different topics, including:

o metal or non-metal properties;
o solid, liquid or gas properties;
o amine or amide properties;
o classification of vertebrates.

CARD SORTS

BASIC IDEA

o Divide students into groups (pairs or 4s work well).
o Provide students with a range of statements related to the subject you are discussing (I find it helpful if these are laminated on card for future use).
o Ask the students to sort the statements under two or three headings, depending upon the subject, e.g. two headings for the first example above would be 'Metal properties' and 'Non-metal properties' (I frequently include these titles as part of the set of cards, in a different colour to make it easier to find at the start of the activity).
o Once the students have sorted their cards then go around the class asking students to 'pick a card' and read it out and then state which heading they have placed it under. This allows the groups to check which ones they have identified correctly, while also giving you an opportunity to discuss any common misconceptions with the class at this early stage.
o Then move on to expand their ideas of the topic involved.

This is another very simple starter activity which I have used with all age ranges and for a variety of different topics.

A concept cartoon consists of cartoon-style characters discussing everyday concepts, e.g. rusting of an iron nail. Each character on the cartoon has a different opinion of the scientific idea involved. These were originally introduced by Stuart Naylor and Brenda Keogh.

The main features of a concept cartoon are that they are a visual representation of a situation, with minimal text. They are designed to stimulate discussion and scientific thinking. They do not necessarily have only one 'right answer', but they tend to come with 'teachers' notes' to help you direct student thinking as required.

BASIC IDEA
o Show a concept cartoon to your students.
o Ask students to discuss these ideas in groups of 4.
o Ask students to feedback their ideas to you.

These cartoons are commercially available so you simply need to photocopy them onto paper or onto an OHT (overhead transparency), or you could scan them into your computer if you are lucky enough to have a projector system in your classroom to show these using ICT. In addition, some concept cartoons are also available in CD ROM format.

This is another excellent starter activity for all year groups. It is relatively simple to prepare and will allow you to access pupils' prior knowledge of a variety of different subjects, including 'neutralization' and 'human organs'.

BASIC IDEA

o Prepare a set of 30 questions related to the topic you are about to introduce.

o Write each question on a separate card.

o Put a star next to the first question.

o Write the answer to the first question on the **second** card.

o Write the answer to the second question on the **third** card.

o Continue until you write the answer to the last question on the first card.

o Give each child in the class a card (you could differentiate the questions at this point).

o Explain that each card has a question and an answer, but the answer does not match the question.

o Identify the student with the star on their card (this is your starting point).

o Ask this student to read out their question.

o Ask students to tell you who has the answer to this question.

o This new student then reads out their answer followed by their question.

o Another student then reads out the correct answer to this question (hopefully).

o Continue until you return to the original student to complete the loop.

As an additional motivation factor, I also distribute 'tokens' to each student. Students then lose their token if they give a wrong answer or miss answering the required question. Anyone with a token left at the end of the session gets a small prize.

You could also redistribute the cards at the end of the lesson to act as a plenary activity. Timing the students on both occasions introduces a competitive element.

This game is designed to help students use and remember some of the more common element symbols. It can also be used to test knowledge of other properties of the elements, e.g. atomic number and atomic mass.

I have used this activity with a variety of year groups through Year 7 to 12. The difference simply lies in the 'questions' you ask, i.e. at Year 7 you may simply give the actual symbol of the element or indeed its name, whereas in Year 12 you may ask something like 'An element with three isotopes, mass 1, 2 and 3'.

REQUIREMENTS
○ 30 different bingo cards
○ Copies of the periodic table
○ Pens
○ Set of 'questions' related to symbols used on cards

MAKING THE BINGO CARDS
I only use the first 20 elements and some of the more common transition metals like copper, zinc, iron, etc. as this makes it easier when writing the statements for each group.

I find that a 4×4 bingo card with 12 elements on it works well. This size allows you to award three 'prizes', for:

○ a completed *row*;
○ a completed *column*; and
○ a *full house*.

A sample bingo card is shown here:

The statements you use will depend on the age group and their knowledge of elements but some examples are:

1 the symbol for the element sodium;
2 the second element in group 7;
3 an element with the atomic number 15.

This is one of my favourite starter activities as the pupils know exactly what to do when they enter the classroom. This activity quickly forms part of the expected routine within the classroom and ensures that effective learning starts as soon as the pupils are settled in their seats. Glossary production not only encourages the pupils to use and understand the scientific terms involved in the unit, but it also provides an excellent opportunity to take the register and deal with any other issues, like homework collection, at the start of the lesson without interfering with the pupils learning.

BASIC IDEA

o At the start of every unit of work my pupils leave 3–4 pages for 'keyword definitions'.

o At the beginning of every lesson they work on producing a glossary of keywords and definitions related to the unit.

o The keywords for each unit are displayed on the walls in my classroom.

o Pupils choose one of these keywords (preferably one we learnt about last lesson) then write it down followed by a simple one-sentence definition.

o They do as many of these as they can at the start of each lesson then we move on to discuss the lesson objectives and content of today's lesson.

o At the end of the unit pupils are asked to complete the glossary for homework.

o This encourages them to use their time wisely at the start of lessons.

Alternatively, I provide the students with a list of the relevant keywords and space to write in the definitions.

KEYWORD/GLOSSARY PRODUCTION

PICTURES

This is another very simple starter activity which is easy to set up. You just need to locate the pictures first and luckily there are many in science resources packs.

BASIC IDEA

Provide students with some pictures related to the topic of the lesson and ask them to discuss what they show. Examples include:

o pictures of the 'same' statue in different environments to show the effect of acid rain;

o pictures of a 'cool pack' and a 'hot pack' to introduce endothermic and exothermic reactions.

This activity can open up good group discussions and can lead on to stimulating classroom discussion on the topics involved.

There are many simple starter activities that involve pupils answering a set of relevant questions or identifying true or false statements, etc. which lend themselves to a whole range of different topics for all age ranges.

I was struck by how 'wasteful' this was in terms of paper and photocopying and now do the following in these situations:

○ laminate the worksheets;
○ give the students waterproof pens (fine OHT pens work well for this) to write their answers thereon;
○ provide damp cloths for students to clean worksheets at end of the starter session;
○ provide a dry tissue so that students can finish cleaning the worksheets, ready for the next use.

This idea also works well for some plenary activities.

USING LAMINATED WORKSHEETS

VIDEO CLIPS

This is a very easy starter activity to set up, the only difficult bit being finding the video clips. This activity not only provides a visual representation of the subject involved but also frequently helps stimulate questions and hence classroom discussions on the subject involved.

I have used this technique with a variety of age ranges and when discussing several different topics, including:

o volcanic eruptions;
o reaction of alkali metals with water (especially as this can demonstrate the highly reactive members of this group).

BASIC IDEA

Play a short video clip or animation of an event or chemical reaction, etc. I then, sometimes, follow this up with a simple demonstration (e.g. show a video clip of all metals reacting with water, then demonstrate the addition of lithium, sodium and potassium to water). Ask for comments or questions, which can lead a classroom discussion on what has been observed, and more importantly ask pupils to explain why things are happening. In the case of alkali metals this leads on to a discussion about ease of losing electrons and the electrostatic pull of a positive nucleus on outer electrons.

Hint: the Internet is a good source of short video clips.

This is a starter activity that can be used with all year groups and while studying a variety of different topics, including human organs, animals (when studying classification), types of acids, elements, etc. The only difficulty is thinking of 30-plus words.

BASIC IDEA

○ Write 30 words on 'post-it' notes related to the topic you are studying.

○ Stick a word onto each pupils' forehead (making sure they do not see their own word).

○ Introduce the topic to the students and encourage them to look around at some of the words on other students' heads to get an idea of the type of words involved.

○ Divide students into groups (pairs or fours work well).

○ Students ask each other questions (make sure they alternate) to determine what their word is; the answer to the questions must only be 'Yes' or 'No'.

I am always surprised about how many scientific questions the students can ask to elucidate their word. Not only does this really get them thinking, the main idea of a starter activity after all, but they also enjoy this 'game'.

This activity can be a little noisy at times and I would recommend that you set a time limit on this of around five minutes. I would also recommend that you have some 'spare' words available for those who guess quickly.

SECTION

3

Effective
discussions

QUESTIONING TECHNIQUES

A variety of different 'brain' research has indicated that no two children learn in the same way (as if we did not know this already). It is imperative that we provide our students with a variety of different learning opportunities, remembering that an enriched learning experience for one child will not necessarily be an enriched experience for another child. We must therefore provide our students with differentiated activities in all areas, including group and classroom discussions.

I use these ideas with all age ranges and vary the activity depending on the subject being discussed and the groups of children involved, while also providing variety in my questioning activities.

○ **Grouping similar ability children together**: this enables all of the students to participate on the same level as each other. I tend to use this if the ideas involved are complex;

○ **Mixed ability grouping**: I tend to use this if the ideas being discussed are less complex. This has the advantage of encouraging peer teaching, as the brighter children tend to explain some of the ideas to other students who are struggling with the concepts involved;

○ **Setting of different questions**: group similar ability children together, then provide each group of pupils with a different set of questions to discuss, depending upon their ability;

○ **Whole-class discussions**: choose your weaker students to answer the easier questions (these may not necessarily be the first questions, to ensure this is not obvious to the other children);

○ **Use of the 'why' question**: my students find the 'why' word the most frustrating, but most of them respond well to the challenge and this really extends the brighter individuals.

There are whole books written on the subject of differentiation, and I have only touched the tip of the iceberg here, but these ideas will give you a starting point to help improve your students' learning experiences in your classroom.

One of the biggest challenges, with pupils of all ages, is to get them to participate in class discussions. There are some children who will do this quite happily while others are, quite simply, mortified if you ask them a question.

I believe that it is very important to get these quieter children involved, as discussing the ideas really does enhance their understanding, and recall, of the concepts involved.

Some of the ideas I use to get my students involved in discussions are:

○ **Use of 'easy' questions**: give your quieter students some of the easier questions until their confidence improves (they will soon become frequent contributors, hopefully);

○ **Traffic lights**: give each student a red, amber and green card (laminating them makes these reusable), ask a question, then ask the students to hold up cards: green if they know the answer, amber if they are unsure and red if they do not know. You then decide who to ask. I sometimes ask the red or amber cards and give them some additional help (this prevents the students holding up red and amber cards all the time), however most students tend to be very truthful during these sessions;

○ **'Yes' or 'no' questions**: for example, will the light bulb in this circuit work? In these cases I ask for a show of hands if they think yes, followed by a show of hands if they think no, making sure all students participate;

○ **A question for every pupil**: some topics lend themselves very well to 30-plus questions, e.g. when discussing the number of electrons, protons and neutrons in atoms I go round the room and ask everyone a question.

Again this is only touching the surface of the techniques available but I hope it stimulates your mind to come up with some other techniques to help you and your students.

WHOLE-CLASS INVOLVEMENT

Dealing with a practical

This is the most fundamental aspect of teaching science. It is imperative that all of your students know how to behave safely in a science laboratory.

There are several situations where I feel it is necessary to discuss safety with your students as discussed below.

AT THE BEGINNING OF YEAR 7

It is absolutely essential that you discuss general safety in the laboratory with your Year 7 students as this is likely to be the first time (apart from an induction day, possibly) that most of them will have even seen a science laboratory. I deal with this in the following way:

- ○ discuss why we have to think about safety;
- ○ discuss the rules we need to have in place to keep us safe;
- ○ give pupils a copy of these rules and have them stick these in their books;
- ○ ask pupils to produce a safety poster depicting one (or more) of the safety rules.

IN THE FIRST LESSON YOU HAVE WITH ANY NEW CLASS

Pupils need reminding of the safety rules, especially after the 'long' summer break.

AT THE BEGINNING OF ANY EXPERIMENT (IN YEAR 7 THROUGH TO YEAR 13)

Pupils need constant reinforcement of the safety rules, however I feel that pupils do not take this on board if I simply repeat the rules. At this stage I ask the students to tell me the essential things we need to do to keep us safe. This also allows you to discuss any safety issues related to the particular experiment involved.

DURING EXPERIMENTS (IF NECESSARY)

If you see any dangerous experimental practices then you must stop the class and discuss this with them immediately.

DEMONSTRATIONS

Demonstrating experiments to pupils is an essential part of any science teacher's work. There are two basic reasons for demonstrating experiments: firstly, some experiments are simply too dangerous to be carried out by the pupils themselves, and secondly, it is often necessary to show pupils how to use a particular piece of equipment.

The first time I demonstrated an experiment I asked the students to gather round to watch and was shocked to discover myself surrounded by pupils who wanted to get as close as possible to the equipment. Not only was this unsafe, but I also felt very uncomfortable and trapped, as there were several pupils literally 'in my face'. Needless to say this did not happen again and I now use a combination of the following ideas whenever I demonstrate experiments:

o **Specific area**: use the same bench in the classroom when carrying out demonstrations wherever possible;
o **Set places**: tell the pupils exactly where you want them to sit or stand during demonstrations (they need to remember these places for next time);
o **Seated or standing?**: have some pupils sat on stools at the front and the others standing behind them, to give all pupils a good view of the demonstration area;
o **Pupils remain seated**: sometimes the demonstration is very visual, e.g. addition of potassium iodide to lead nitrate produces a bright yellow precipitate. In these cases holding up the apparatus so that everyone can see while you are adding the reactants together works well. In addition to this you could take the reaction vessel round to each table so that the pupils can get a closer look at the reaction.

The technique that I use depends mainly on the demonstration involved, but the layout of your room will also have an effect on your choices.

IDEA

23

SETTING UP A PRACTICAL 1: COLLECTING EQUIPMENT *EN MASSE*

This method is the least time consuming for yourself and the laboratory technician. It also has the advantage of allowing the students to collect equipment 'quickly'.

BASIC IDEA

o Set out all equipment required for the practical on a side bench or trolley.
o Divide pupils into groups (3s or 4s work well).
o Pupils collect equipment from this area at the start of the practical session.
o Pupils then get on with the practical.

This method is simplicity itself but can be dangerous if a 'mob' situation develops. It does, however, work well with older students who have been trained how to collect equipment sensibly over the years.

This method allows the pupils to collect the required equipment quickly while alleviating the 'mob' situation.

BASIC IDEA

o Set up equipment around the room, e.g. a tray of beakers at the front of the room, a tray of measuring cylinders in the middle of the room, etc.
o Divide pupils into groups for the practical.
o Pupils decide who is collecting which equipment.
o Pupils collect equipment from the relevant areas.
o Pupils then carry out the experiment.

This method requires a little more preparation than Idea 23 in terms of setting out the equipment, but less than some of the other ideas discussed here. It can also sometimes lead to confusion for students as they don't know exactly where anything is, but they usually sort it out quite quickly, with some direction from the teacher and other class members.

SETTING UP A PRACTICAL 2: EQUIPMENT SPREAD AROUND THE ROOM

This method can be very time consuming and involves a lot of teacher interaction.

BASIC IDEA

○ Set out equipment at the side of the room or on trolleys.
○ Divide the pupils into groups for the practical.
○ Allocate each member of the group a number.
○ Discuss with the class the equipment required for the experiment.
○ As pupils identify a chemical or piece of equipment ask a pupil from each group to collect the required equipment, using the allocated numbers.
○ Continue until each group has all necessary equipment.

This is an excellent way of introducing Year 7 pupils to ideas about how to collect equipment at the start of a practical session. It also provides a very good opportunity for you to discuss the safety issues related to each piece of equipment. I have also used this method to highlight the need for group members to collect different pieces of equipment and chemicals to ensure efficient use of time during practical sessions.

This method can also be very time consuming, but it does work well if combined with another relevant activity, e.g. reading through instructions for experiment, drawing a results table, etc.

BASIC IDEA

o Set out the equipment on a side bench or trolley.
o Divide the pupils into groups for the practical session.
o Ask pupils to discuss who is getting which equipment for the experiment.
o Pupils then read instructions or record relevant information in their books in silence (e.g. theory behind experiment, results table, etc.).
o The teacher directs one group at a time to collect the required equipment and then return to their desks and continue with the silent task set.
o Once all equipment is allocated groups can start the experiment at the teacher's direction.

I find this method works very well with all year groups and results in an ordered start to the practical session.

SETTING UP A PRACTICAL 4:
ONE GROUP AT A TIME

SETTING UP A PRACTICAL 5: SETS OF EQUIPMENT

This is simply the best method of allocating equipment to the students, in my opinion.

It works well with all age groups, although I tend only to use this for experiments that require lots of different chemicals due to the issues discussed below.

BASIC IDEA

o Put all necessary equipment for the experiment into trays.
o Pupils then simply collect a tray, one per group, at the beginning of the practical session.

This method is however very time consuming for either yourself or the laboratory technician as it involves collecting and sorting required equipment into approximately 8 trays per class. This also requires more space in preparation rooms, which is often a problem in areas that are already short of space. A good compromise here is to provide the chemicals in sets. Ice cream tubs work well here. Then students can collect glassware, etc. from trays using one of the other methods described.

One of the biggest issues for a science teacher is making sure all of the equipment is returned correctly at the end of an experiment. In my early months of teaching I often found myself clearing up after a class, as my next class was arriving, not exactly the best start to any lesson, let alone the stress this added to my day. While reflecting on this I remembered an excellent piece of advice given to me by a very wise science teacher during my training:

> 'Always leave at least five minutes at the end of the lesson to check that equipment has been put away and that your sinks are clear!'

I also realized that I needed to train my pupils to put away equipment correctly. Some of the ideas I implement include:

○ start training early (beginning of Year 7);
○ explain the importance of putting equipment away correctly;
   ○ safety;
   ○ need to be available for other classes, etc.;
○ discuss how to put equipment away, reminding pupils to:
   ○ rinse out equipment if needed;
   ○ return equipment to the correct areas;
   ○ make sure equipment is put away neatly, etc.;
○ leave time at the end of the practical to check everything is away correctly (you can always fill this time with a class discussion once everything is correct);
○ make sure students see you checking the equipment;
○ constantly reinforce these ideas;
○ do not move on to next activity until you are happy that everything is OK (this works even better if the lesson ends on a break, as you can simply leave the 'tidying up' until then).

My students learn very quickly to put equipment away neatly. I always find that there are a couple of students who tend to check, and correct, before I have a chance to do so.

CLEARING AWAY APPARATUS

VIRTUAL EXPERIMENTS

Over the years I have sometimes found that it is impossible to carry out some experiments. This is either because the experiments are too dangerous (reaction of some alkali metals with water), the facilities needed are not available at the required time, or some individuals in my class present a safety hazard themselves and part of my risk assessment for the lesson may include isolating these individuals while the other pupils carry out the intended experiment.

Virtual experiments go some way to helping resolve these problems. They can either act as an alternative activity for the isolated individuals, or they could simply act as a 'safe' alternative for the whole class to participate in. Virtual experiments also have the advantage of requiring little setting up, something that can take a surprising amount of time, and subsequently allowing the students more time to carry out the actual investigation.

Virtual experiments are available from a range of sources, including the Internet. The basic requirements for this activity therefore include computer access and instructions on how to find the required experiment on the computer system. You may also wish to discuss the workings of the virtual experiment with the students before they start using the programme.

In my early years of teaching this was the one question I dreaded hearing. I found myself 'running' around the classroom like a 'headless chicken' trying to answer all groups' questions, great for the stress levels!

Some of the ideas I have since implemented in my classroom to help resolve this are listed below (I now have time to actually talk to the children about what they are doing, a much more productive use of my time, and theirs):

○ provide pupils with a worksheet containing step by step instructions;
○ display instructions for the experiment on the board;
○ demonstrate how to do the experiment before the pupils have a go;
○ plan the experiment as a whole class and then let pupils carry out the experiment;
○ encourage pupils to make notes on the procedure;
○ draw diagrams on the board (or on a worksheet) showing the steps involved.

I often find that a combination of these works well, but it does really depend on the children you have in front of you. I still find myself having to remind pupils to read the sheet or board, but this is much easier than a full-blown explanation repeated over and over again.

WHAT DO I DO NEXT MISS?

LETTING THEM JUST GET ON WITH IT

As teachers we can be guilty of trying to control everything that goes on inside our classrooms, especially during practical sessions, something I was definitely guilty of until recently.

Over the last few years, however, I have learnt to take a few steps back and let my students simply get on with the task in hand, especially when I am teaching the older children. Recently, I have taken to standing at the back, or front, of my classroom while pupils carry out a practical activity. I find a position where I can scan the whole class and see exactly what is going on in all groups.

I believe this implies an element of trust on my part, as well as providing a degree of freedom for the students. This has resulted in my pupils feeling more secure in their practical abilities and hence has improved their learning in my classroom. In addition to this the pupils know exactly where I am and come and ask for help if they need it, a much better distribution of my help in my opinion.

This 'taking a step back' also allows me to observe the whole class and assess their progress in several areas, including their practical skills and participation in practical sessions. It soon becomes obvious who the experimental 'observers' are and I can then encourage them to get more involved in these sessions.

Give it a go – you'll be surprised by the results.

Fun class activities

This is an excellent experiment that, if carried out carefully, produces the whole pH scale in a test tube. It can be used with any age group whenever you are discussing the pH scale or neutralization reactions.

REQUIREMENTS

- o 2 grams of sodium hydroxide in a test tube (to reduce safety hazards)
- o Universal indicator
- o Distilled water
- o Ethanoic acid
- o Measuring cylinder
- o Test tube rack

INSTRUCTIONS

1 Place the test tube in a test tube rack (works best if test tube at an angle).
2 Add 2 cm³ of distilled water to dissolve the hydroxide.
3 Add a few drops of universal indicator.
4 Add 2 cm³ of ethanoic acid **very slowly** to the test tube (this works best if drizzled down the side of the tube – a dropping pipette may help here); you should see very little fizz if adding at an appropriate speed.
5 Add a second 2 cm³ of ethanoic acid to the test tube as above.
6 Observe the test tube contents.

This gives a great opportunity to assess the manipulation skills of your students as it only works if they have been very careful during the addition of the acid, while also providing an excellent visualization of the complete pH scale.

I tend to use this activity with my Year 10 students after they have completed their Year 10 external examination as a special treat, although you could also use this to investigate the properties of solids and liquids.

REQUIREMENTS

- ○ Cornflour (a cupful per group)
- ○ Water
- ○ Food colouring (optional)
- ○ Large container for mixing (ice cream tubs work well)
- ○ Small plastic objects (e.g. 'lego' bricks)
- ○ Soap (for washing up students afterwards!)

INSTRUCTIONS

1 Make sure the tables are covered with newspaper as this experiment is **very** messy.
2 Place cornflour in container.
3 Add a few drops of food colouring (any colour you like).
4 **Slowly** add water and mix with fingers, until it feels like a liquid when you are mixing it slowly, but does not splash when you tap the surface with your finger, so a bit solid (be careful not to add too much water).
5 Investigate the properties of this substance.

INVESTIGATING THE PROPERTIES OF THE SUBSTANCE

- ○ Stir the mixture **slowly** with your finger.
- ○ Stir the mixture **quickly**.
- ○ Rest your finger on the surface and slowly push your finger to the bottom of the container.
- ○ Try to pull your finger out **quickly**.
- ○ Pick up some of the mixture and squeeze it.
- ○ Stop squeezing and let it drip through your fingers.
- ○ Try to make a ball by rolling some of it in your hands.
- ○ Stop rolling – what happens?
- ○ Place some small objects on the surface of the substance.

Once the students have had an opportunity to play with this substance I often ask them to discuss whether it is a solid or a liquid. This not only enhances their understanding of solid and liquid properties but also encourages great debating skills and is great fun!

IDEA
34

I use this activity as part of the A-level chemistry course where it is used to help explain hydrogen bonding between polymer chains, although it can also be used lower down the school to show unusual properties of polymers, or even more simply the properties of solids and liquids.

REQUIREMENTS
o Polystyrene cups
o Wooden sticks (e.g. lolly sticks)
o Food colouring (optional)
o Sodium borate solution – 4%
o Poly(ethenol) solution – 4%
o Measuring cylinders
o Gloves

INSTRUCTIONS
Warning: 'slime' can stain carpets and remove paint!

1 Measure 50 cm³ of poly(ethenol) in a measuring cylinder and add to the polystyrene cup.
2 Add a few drops of food colouring (any colour you like, although green is popular, you can imagine why).
3 Add 10 cm³ of sodium borate solution, and mix with wooden stick.
4 Investigate the properties of this substance – make sure you wear gloves.

Some of my students (and lab. technicians) have been able to get this amount of slime to stretch far enough to reach from one end of my lab to the other! This takes great care and patience, however, as the slime will 'break' if handled incorrectly. Other activities involve watching the effect of gravity on the slime and placing the slime over writing in water soluble ink.

THE THEORY
The borate ions form cross-linkages between the poly(ethenol) chains, resulting in stronger linkages than the original intermolecular forces present between the polymer chains themselves. These 'new' linkages are hydrogen bonding between the OH groups on the borate ion, $[B(OH)_4]^-$, and the OH groups on the poly(ethenol) chains, which result in the solid and liquid properties observed.

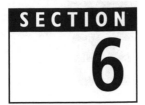

Just biology

TEACHING ADAPTATION – MAKING A 'SURVIVAL' GAME

This activity is more time consuming that most and will take several hours of lesson time, but it usually produces some excellent work and gives pupils a great understanding of animals' and plants' adaptations to their environment. It is also an excellent activity to carry out after a school trip to the zoo.

RESOURCES

o Variety of books on different animals and plants.
o Poster materials, plastic cups, pipe cleaners, glitter, glue, etc.

BASIC IDEA

Aim: to produce a board game.

o The game must be based around a single animal or plant and its environment, although other organisms that live in the same environment can be incorporated.
o The game must have some reference to how the animal or plant survives, as well as how it is adapted to its environment.
o The pupils first need to research the animal or plant they have chosen; I usually ask for a short bullet point summary of their findings at this point (they may wish to print off some pictures from the Internet for later use).
o They then need to construct their game using any resources available to them – it is useful to get them to think about board games they have previously played.
o A simple example could be based on the lifestyles of a mouse using snakes and ladders as the reference game, although your brighter students may wish to include questions to allow them to move around the board or get around obstacles, rather than just using dice.
o Pupils then swap and play each other's games.
o Pupils then rate the games they played and feed back to the manufacturers.

This activity does not only allow the students to think about adaptation but it also allows them to express their creativity. It also enhances their evaluative skills when they feed back to the manufacturer about their game.

This is a fun activity which highlights pupil misconceptions about the position of organs in the human body, and is an excellent way of accessing pupil's prior knowledge on this subject.

I find that this activity works best with the younger children because they tend to be less inhibited than their older peers, although it can be adapted for older students by providing them with a body outline.

RESOURCES (PER GROUP)

o Body sized pieces of paper (lining paper from your local DIY store works well for this).
o A volunteer.
o Pencils.
o List of organs (I usually write these on the board).

BASIC IDEA

o Divide class into small groups (4s–6s work well).
o Volunteer lies on 'body sized' piece of paper on the floor.
o Other members of the group draw around the volunteer, using pencils, to produce a body outline (do not use marker pens as these may damage clothes).
o The volunteer and other group members then draw in organs as per the list given.
o Pupils then feed back to the whole class by holding up their 'bodies'.
o Other groups then 'challenge' any positions they disagree with.
o Teacher corrects pupils as required.
o Class then look at a model of the human torso to show the relative positions of the organs discussed.

This activity is not only fun but also stimulates a large amount of discussion within groups regarding the position of the human organs, while also providing a pictorial representation to help those visual learners.

This activity can be extended by asking the pupils to judge the size and shapes of the organs as well. Alternatively, for lower ability pupils you could provide them with laminated pictures of the required organs to place in their body shapes.

This is a topic that some teachers find difficult. The following idea is one I use to help avoid some potentially embarrassing questions, while also allowing my students to ask the questions they wish to ask but are frequently too embarrassed to do so.

I use this idea when I introduce this topic to my Year 7s in the summer term, although it is suitable for all age ranges.

BASIC IDEA

○ I provide a 'secret questions box' in my room while teaching this unit.

○ I tell the students that they can add questions to this box at the beginning of each lesson during this unit (I tend to hold this box while I let the students into the room to allow them to add questions with the minimum of fuss).

○ I then leave some time at the end of the last lesson of the unit to open the box and read out and answer these questions.

Before opening the box in front of the pupils I sort the questions and remove the 'less appropriate' ones to avoid any awkward situations. I also tend to have some spare questions that I don't answer, due to lack of time, so that the students do not realize that these questions have been removed. In fairness, there tends not to be many questions that require this treatment.

While teaching this unit I often found I was faced with some very unpleasant slang words for parts of the male and female reproductive systems. This activity is one way I have found to deal with these words, with the minimum of embarrassment on my part, while also allowing the students to learn the correct biological terms.

I use this activity when introducing this topic to my Year 7s, although it is suitable for all age ranges.

BASIC IDEA

o Divide students into group (3s or 4s).

o Provide them with a large piece of poster paper and pens.

o Ask them to divide paper into two and label one side 'female' and the other 'male'.

o Ask pupils to write down **any** words they know for reproductive organs (explain that they will not be in trouble at this stage for using incorrect terms).

o Discuss the correct biological parts of the male and female anatomy and ask students to cross off any other names for this particular part (I tend to combine this with the labelling of biological diagrams with the correct terms).

o Ask if they have any words left and ask them to **point** them out to you (to discourage use of these 'slang' terms).

o Let them know what the term refers to (this sometimes requires the help of a scientific diagram that you can ask them to point to as I am surprised by some of the terms and genuinely do not know what they are referring to).

o Discuss with the students the need to learn the correct terms and the need to use these at all times in our lessons.

I have found this activity very effective and tend to hear very few, or no, 'slang' words during my reproduction lessons after this point.

TEACHING SEXUAL REPRODUCTION – AVOIDING THOSE 'SLANG' WORDS

Just chemistry

ATOMIC PEOPLE

It is almost impossible to allow your students to see actual particles (unless you are lucky enough to have access to a very powerful electron microscope!).

One of the ways I get around this problem is to ask my students to imagine themselves as atoms (or particles). This activity works best with the younger children, although I have also used it with some of my older students, depending upon the group.

I then use these 'atomic people' to represent a variety of different concepts including:

○ **Kinetic theory**: arrange atomic people in patterns to represent solids, liquids and gases. Can also be used to represent relative movement of these particles;

○ **Collision theory**: mix up 'atomic people' representing different particles (I give them different coloured cards), ask them to move around and count how many collisions they have with the required particle for a reaction. Repeat using a different combination of particles, e.g. more water and less reactant particles, and compare number of collisions to show less reactions in a dilute situation (hopefully!);

○ **Balancing equations**: e.g. reaction of methane with oxygen. Discuss word equation and symbols of reactants, then ask for seven volunteers and provide each student with an A4 card showing an atom. I use a different colour for each different atom here ($1 \times C$, $4 \times H$, $2 \times O$). Volunteers should join together to form methane and oxygen. The volunteers can rearrange themselves, with help of class mates and will hopefully realize that they do not have enough oxygen atoms. Ask for two more volunteers and repeat the process – it should now work.

This activity is very versatile and I am sure you could think of lots of other situations where it could help in your teaching.

I personally had trouble as a child remembering the different 'S' words related to solubility. I am therefore not surprised when my students get these mixed up.

The words involved are:

o Solubility;
o Solvent;
o Solute;
o Solution;
o Saturated;
o Insoluble;
o Soluble;
o Dissolve.

Some of the ideas I have tried to help my students with this are listed below:

o **Written descriptions**: ask students to write a description of how to make a salt solution, using as many of the solubility words as possible. Then show them a 'correct' version;
o **Keyword descriptions** (or posters): simple definitions for each word can be written (or use the keyword poster activity described in Idea 59);
o **Card sort**: give pupils a set of cards with definitions and keywords and ask them to match them together;
o **Provide definitions**: then ask pupils to tell you the correct scientific term;
o **Spelling test**: a great activity whenever you introduce a new scientific word;
o **Pairs games**: see Idea 56 for instructions on how to do this;
o **Group quizzes**: encourages pupils to discuss the ideas and hence helps them remember the terms.

The main issue here is to ensure repetition so that your students have the opportunity to get these words fixed firmly in their minds.

These activities are also useful when dealing with other situations where you introduce a large number of similar words, e.g. when discussing the parts of plant and animal cells.

IDEA 41

Pupils often struggle to use the collision theory effectively to explain rates of reaction. They frequently find it difficult to remember why the rate of reaction increases or decreases under certain conditions.

I use this activity with my Year 10s to consolidate their knowledge after we have finished looking at the unit of work on rates of reaction, although it also makes an excellent revision exercise for Year 11s in the summer term.

INSTRUCTIONS

1 Divide an A3 size piece of paper into sections as shown opposite.
2 Produce a comic strip on the effect of concentration on rates of reaction.
3 Draw a comical picture in each of the eight large boxes (this could simply involve 'round' particles with faces).
4 Add a short explanation in the smaller boxes (could describe the journey of a particle as it tries to react with other particles in concentrated and dilute situations – example statements are shown opposite).
5 Include a title and add colour.
6 Repeat with other effects, e.g. temperature, surface area, catalyst.

This activity provides an opportunity for the students' imaginations to run free while also providing them with a visual stimuli to remember this knowledge in the examinations. It also provides you with some excellent display materials to help provide a stimulating environment in your classroom.

I provide prizes for the best presentation and the funniest comic strips.

This idea can also be adapted for other subjects including the history of metals, pollination, respiration and distillation of crude oil.

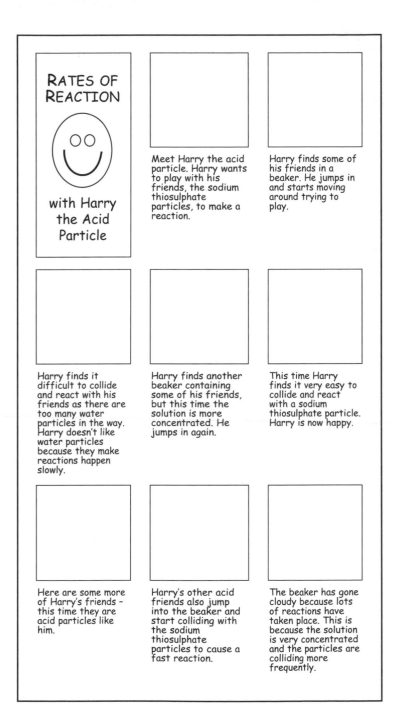

RATES OF REACTION

with Harry the Acid Particle

Meet Harry the acid particle. Harry wants to play with his friends, the sodium thiosulphate particles, to make a reaction.

Harry finds some of his friends in a beaker. He jumps in and starts moving around trying to play.

Harry finds it difficult to collide and react with his friends as there are too many water particles in the way. Harry doesn't like water particles because they make reactions happen slowly.

Harry finds another beaker containing some of his friends, but this time the solution is more concentrated. He jumps in again.

This time Harry finds it very easy to collide and react with a sodium thiosulphate particle. Harry is now happy.

Here are some more of Harry's friends – this time they are acid particles like him.

Harry's other acid friends also jump into the beaker and start colliding with the sodium thiosulphate particles to cause a fast reaction.

The beaker has gone cloudy because lots of reactions have taken place. This is because the solution is very concentrated and the particles are colliding more frequently.

IDEA

42

One of the most difficult concepts in chemistry is getting pupils to visualize 3D shapes when presented with 2D diagrams. We frequently use molecular modelling kits when looking at molecular shapes but I have found the following activity more effective and a lot more fun.

I tend to use this activity with my A-level chemists after we have discussed the theory of electron repulsion and molecular shapes, although it could also act as a fun extension activity for some of your gifted and talented Year 11s (I simply adapt the instructions to say which molecules the shapes represent).

REQUIREMENTS (PER GROUP)

o Three 'long' balloons (the type used to make balloon animals).
o Instruction worksheet.
o A healthy heart (as their will no doubt be some large 'pops').
o Pins for popping balloons.

EXAMPLE INSTRUCTIONS

1 Blow up and tie the balloons (do not blow them up too hard).
2 Twist a balloon in the middle (this now represents two atoms joined by a single bond) – this produces a linear shape as expected!
3 Twist a second balloon in the middle and join to the first balloon, making sure you twist the balloons around each other several times, to give a tetrahedral shape – how many electron pairs does this represent?
4 Twist a third balloon in the middle and add to the tetrahedral – what shape have you produced?
5 Use a pin to pop one of the 'balloon halves' to give five bonds. This part only works if you have done the twisting correctly, otherwise you will end up with a tetrahedral again. What shape is this?

The students will then take great pleasure in popping all of the balloons (they always succeed in making me jump several times despite the fact that I know they will do this).

The Haber process is one of the important industrial processes taught as part of many science syllabuses (although the following ideas could be adapted to teach other industrial processes as well). The students often find this part of the course challenging due to the large amount of new information presented to them. The following are ideas to help teach this industrial process:

o briefly introduce the Haber process to the students;
o ask students to research details of the Haber process using a range of books, and a set of questions. Then write bullet point notes (this could be set as a homework activity);
o provide pupils with a set of cards containing a range of statements about the Haber process and its products to help consolidate knowledge. Have them sort these cards into true and false statements using their heads only, then after a few minutes allow them to use their notes.

Examples of some of the statements I have used are listed below:

1 The Haber process uses nitrogen as a starting material.
2 Ammonia is an odourless gas.
3 The Haber process was named after Fred Haber.
4 Ammonium nitrate is a fertilizer.

I always put in at least one tricky question to keep students on their toes. For example:

$$N_2 + 3H_2 \rightarrow 2NH_3$$

The word equation for the Haber process is

Most students identify this statement as true but note that it is not the 'word' equation, it is the 'symbol' equation. You usually hear several debates about these statements and so this also enhances debating skills.

Interactive CD ROMs are also available to show this process visually, which helps enhance learning further.

TEACHING THE HABER PROCESS

SECTION
8

Just physics

IDEA 44

I have frequently found that students find it difficult to distinguish between the three types of heat transfer – conduction, convection and radiation. The following activity has helped some of my students get to grips with these ideas and is suitable for all age ranges, although it works best with younger children.

BASIC IDEA

o Line students up next to each other like particles in a solid (you can use a whole class or a small group).
o Give the first student in the line a tennis ball.
o Explain that the pupils are particles in a solid and the tennis ball is the heat energy.
o Explain to the students that the aim is to get the ball to the other end of the line.

There are three ways this could happen (to ensure all three ways happen you may need to direct students at points):

1 pass the object from one 'particle' to the next, until the tennis ball gets to the other end (represents conduction);
2 a 'particle' takes the tennis ball to the 'particle' at the end of line (convection);
3 a 'particle' throws the tennis ball to the 'particle' at the end of line (radiation).

This helps pupils to visualize what is happening to the heat energy and why particles are important. Then go on to discuss this theory further, including why you cannot stop heat loss by radiation.

One of the difficult concepts when teaching electrical circuits involves looking at the differences between series and parallel circuits. The following activity is one that I have used with my Year 7 students when this concept is introduced to them, although it would be suitable for older children as well, depending upon the group involved.

BASIC IDEA

o Use tables and chairs to set up a some alleyways representing a series circuit.

o Mark out the battery terminals on one of the desks using chalk.

o Ask pupils to imagine they are electrons (electricity) and 'walk' round this circuit. Remind them that they need to start at the negative terminal and head back to the positive terminal of the battery (they should observe that there is only one route for them to follow).

o Rearrange the tables and chairs to produce alleyways representing a parallel circuit.

o Ask pupils to 'walk' around this new circuit. Stop them when some choices have been made and discuss the relevance of this (they should observe that in a parallel circuit the electrons have more than one route to follow – probability indicates that half of the electrons will go one way and the other half will 'choose' the other route, providing the resistance is identical in each 'branch').

o Back this up with some diagrams of circuits on the board.

This activity can be a bit of a nightmare in terms of rearrangement of furniture. Alternatively, you could clear a space in the middle of the floor and draw large circuit diagrams on the floor using chalk and then ask the students to stay 'on the lines'. Or you might use string and take the students outside onto the playing field to carry out this activity.

SERIES AND PARALLEL CIRCUITS

I have often found that pupils sometimes have difficulty visualizing the planets' distance from us and the sun. This activity is designed to help them with this, while also highlighting some other issues, including the relative 'closeness' of the first four planets related to the other five, and the relative sizes of the planets.

REQUIREMENTS

- ○ Nine large planet cards, with bulldog clips, each showing the planet's name and its distance from the sun.
- ○ A very long piece of string (at least 60 metres).
- ○ Long measuring tape.
- ○ A playground or field.
- ○ 30 small cards with individual planets' names thereon to give to the pupils (the number of cards for each planet should relate to the relative diameter of the planet, e.g. Jupiter = 11 cards, whereas Earth = 1 card)

BASIC IDEA

- ○ Show students data showing the various distances of the planets from the sun.
- ○ Ask students to decide on a suitable scale for the playground to display these distances (100 million km = 1 metre works well).
- ○ Work out the distance from the sun in metres for each planet as a class.
- ○ Outside, attach string to a fixed object (the sun) and then attach 'large planet cards' to string at correct distances.
- ○ Look at the distances and discuss the relevant issues.
- ○ Give each pupil a small planet card and ask them to form straight lines next to the planet that matches their card.
- ○ Discuss relative diameters of planets with students.
- ○ Return to the classroom to consolidate ideas.

This activity is suitable for all age groups but does present some issues in terms of classroom management so choose your groups carefully for this, but the pupils will really appreciate this opportunity and it is well worth doing if possible.

This is an activity that I have used when teaching forces and motion. The activity investigates inertia (which is not really required for GCSE science, although this is an excellent extension activity for your gifted and talented students while also providing a fun investigation that children of all abilities will enjoy, although some will struggle to understand the theory involved).

BASIC IDEA

o Place a piece of card on top of a beaker (or a plastic cup).
o Place a two pence coin on top of the card.
o Remove the card, without moving the coin in the direction of the applied force, so that the coin ends up in the container.
o Investigate the effect of different sized coins and different sizes or shapes of card.

Pupils usually start by pulling the card away very slowly – this does not work! The card needs to be removed very quickly. I have found the best way is to flick the card from one corner and I would suggest you practise this before introducing this activity to your students so that you can prove that it is possible.

THE THEORY

If the card is removed quickly then there is insufficient force to overcome the inertia of the coin and it does not move in the direction of the applied force. (Inertia is the resistance an object has to a change in its state of motion.) The only quantity that should affect the amount of inertia is the mass of the object. The higher the mass, the larger the inertia, so your students should find this easier with heavier coins (providing they do not bend the card).

This activity can be a bit of an issue in terms of classroom management, lots of cards being 'flicked' around, so choose your groups wisely.

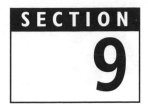

Scientific investigations

IDEA 48

CONTINUOUS SKILL BUILDING

I strongly believe that it is important to start teaching investigation skills early. Most pupils arrive at secondary school with a basic understanding of scientific investigations and it is important that these skills are built upon gradually and at every opportunity.

It is essential that all units of work in science should include an element of scientific investigation and that such investigations should be coordinated so that every student in the school has developed all of the appropriate skills by the time they need to complete coursework for their GCSEs. With this in mind, some examples that my department use are listed below (although there are obviously lots of other opportunities to enhance investigative skills):

○ Year 7 – the investigations unit looks at carrying out experiments and analysing data appropriately;
○ Year 8 – lemonade investigation – looks at the use of preliminary work to inform a plan;
○ Year 9 – metal and acid experiment – looks at obtaining quantitative data and recording multiple results on one graph;
○ Year 10 – disappearing cross experiment – looks at choosing appropriate equipment.

This is another skill that does not just develop on its own – it needs to be taught to pupils. Again, this came as quite a shock to me in my early years of teaching but, upon reflection, was not surprising and I have since learnt never to assume anything. I now take every opportunity, especially with my Year 7 students, to discuss how to use pieces of equipment correctly.

The best way I have found of teaching equipment manipulation skills is:

○ demonstrate the use of equipment to the students;
○ point out any pitfalls as you come across them;
○ encourage students to ask questions during the demonstration;
○ constantly ask them their opinions on 'what we do next';
○ occasionally do something blatantly wrong to get them 'challenging' you;
○ draw a large diagram on the board to discuss fine detail, e.g. the meniscus of water when using measuring cylinders, etc.

Interestingly, while I was teaching my Year 11 students how to use a burette recently, I had a student tell me, quite insistently, that the surface of water was totally flat and that there was no such thing as a meniscus. She only believed me when I filled a measuring cylinder and showed her this phenomenon. She was totally shocked and said that she had used a measuring cylinder on several occasions before this and had not 'seen' the meniscus – this makes you think about how accurate her measurements were and certainly proved to me the need to teach pupils how to use equipment correctly, and to constantly reinforce these ideas.

EQUIPMENT MANIPULATION

WRITING A METHOD

I always find it interesting that students find it difficult to write a method for an experiment including all the necessary details of what they did or intend to do. Whether they have already carried out the experiment or are actually planning what to do, many students struggle with this task, although the former situation does tend to result in better methods.

One of the ideas I have used to get across the importance of this is as follows:

o ask students to write a method to describe 'how to make a cup of tea';
o choose pupils to read out their plans, while you do exactly what they say;
o challenge anything you do not understand, some examples include:
  o 'plug the kettle in' – my response would be 'to where, and which part of the kettle?';
  o 'plug the kettle into the wall' – this results in much hilarity as I try to push the whole kettle into the wall;
  o 'fill the kettle', my response 'with what, and do you really mean fill?' etc.;
o point out the things they should have said with the help of the rest of the class.

I have to admit to getting a little sarcastic during these sessions and the children often find my reactions, especially my very confused face, hilarious, so choose your students carefully for this and make sure they realize that you are not 'having a go'. I also make sure I choose several students and tend to swap from one individual to another to help alleviate the pressure as well.

Pupils often find it difficult to know exactly what to include in all parts of investigation write-ups. I have used the following activity to give pupils an opportunity to see how a method should be written. This activity is an excellent introduction to method writing in Year 7, but is also suitable for your lower ability children.

BASIC IDEA

o Pupils carry out an experiment.

o Provide pupils with an incomplete method (I tend to write the method myself then look for appropriate words to remove).

o Include a list of the missing words.

o Pupils then fill in the missing words to complete the method.

If you wish to make this a little more challenging then you could leave out the missing words or larger parts of sentences. Ultimately, you want your students to be able to write methods themselves so I would only suggest using this on one or two occasions, just so that the students get an idea of what is expected.

Although this can be time consuming initially, you will find this very productive in helping your younger and lower ability students improve their method writing, and you could always use the same sheet in future years.

This also works very well when looking at writing conclusions.

FILL IN THE GAPS EXERCISES

SECTION 10

Plenary activities

IDEA 52

ANAGRAMS

This activity helps students visualize, and learn to spell, some of the important scientific words, as well as being seen as a fun activity. It can be used with any year group and when discussing any aspect of science.

BASIC IDEA

Make a list of related words for the lesson (or set of lessons) involved. Scramble the letters in the words and give this as a list to the students. Then ask the students to identify what the words are.

Examples of when I have used this include when looking at:

○ common chemicals used in reactions;
○ planets of the solar system;
○ acidic and alkaline substances;
○ parts of a cell.

I usually give prizes or credits to the student (or group of students) who get all of the words in the shortest time.

Crosswords and wordsearches make very good plenary activities and can involve very little preparation as there are plenty available in science resources as well as on the Internet. They are suitable for all year groups and allow simple differentiation to be carried out within the class, as the only difference would be the words involved and possibly how complicated the clues are.

BASIC IDEA

Provide the pupils with a crossword or wordsearch containing some of the keywords that have been discussed as part of the lesson (or set of lessons) and ask them to complete it as quickly as possible. I tend to give prizes for the first person to complete the activity.

EXTENSION

To make this activity more challenging for your more gifted pupils you could ask them to produce their own crossword using the keywords from the lesson. This not only means they need to think what the keywords are but also what they mean. A simpler version of this could be to produce their own wordsearch, as this only requires the keywords, not the definitions. Provide the pupils with squared paper to help with the layout of these puzzles.

CROSSWORDS AND WORDSEARCHES

HOT SEAT QUESTIONING

This activity is suitable for all age ranges but needs to be handled sympathetically as it involves putting the focus on one student only in the classroom, which some students will struggle with. If this is common practice in your lessons, however, the students will become less embarrassed as they know they are not the only ones to take part in this type of activity. To make this less of an issue you could consider choosing a pair, or larger group, of students to work together to answer the questions.

BASIC IDEA

- Choose a pupil to sit in a seat (or stand), at the front of the classroom. There are several ways of choosing your first 'victim' including:
  - asking for volunteers;
  - choosing a student who is a regular contributor to discussions (as they are more confident);
  - choosing a student who has shown a real interest in the subject of the lesson;
  - choosing a student who does not always pay attention to the lesson carefully (they will pay more attention in future!);
  - choosing a number and then using the register to identify which student corresponds to this number.
- The pupil is then asked several questions related to the lesson (or set of lessons). The questions can come from yourself (best to start with a few) and from the other pupils (although they **must** know the correct answer themselves).

I tend to give the hot seat person a few sweets as a 'kitty'. If they answer questions correctly then they get to keep the sweets, though every time they answer a question incorrectly they have to give up a sweet to the pupil who asked the question, only if the questioner can give the correct answer. If neither can give the correct answer then the sweets get returned to me.

This activity is designed to help pupils remember items in a particular order and is suitable for all age ranges. A mnemonic is a rhyme (or formula) designed to help the brain remember details. The word comes from the Greek *mnemonikós*, which refers to the mind. The theory behind mnemonics is that most people find it easier to remember a rhyme, especially if it is a comical one, rather than a list of 'unrelated' words.

BASIC IDEA

o Pupils list the items being discussed in order.
o They then take the first letter of each item and write these down in order.
o Pupils then make up a mnemonic to help them remember the order of items using the first letters identified (the first letters must be in the correct order for this to work).

For example, two mnemonics designed to help pupils remember the order of the planets of the solar system are:

My Very Easy Method Just Speeds Up Naming Planets

My Very Excellent Mum Just Served Us Nine Pizzas

Mercury, Venus, Earth, Mars, Jupiter, Saturn, Uranus, Neptune, Pluto

Other topics I have found this useful for include:

o reactivity series of metals;
o taxonomy;
o the Kreb's cycle;
o colours of light spectrum.

To help extend this idea, and to give it a visual twist to enhance learning even further, I have often asked pupils to design a poster showing the scientific list of items and their mnemonic, along with some suitable pictures.

PAIRS GAME

This game is designed to help students use some of the important scientific terms introduced in a lesson (or set of lessons), as well as helping them to remember the definitions. I have used this activity with a variety of year groups, through Year 7 to 13. The difference simply lies in the 'scientific terms' and definitions you use.

MAKING THE PAIRS CARDS
- ○ Write keywords related to the unit being studied onto individual cards (A7 or A8 size works well).
- ○ Write a definition for each keyword on separate cards.
- ○ Produce as many sets as groups in the class – I tend to make each set a different colour (this works well with 3–4 pupils per group – I usually make 8 sets).
- ○ Laminate cards, if time allows (better if you intend to reuse them).

PLAYING THE GAME
- ○ Give out the sets of cards and ask pupils to spread these out on the table with the writing face down.
- ○ Pupils take it in turns to turn over two cards. If the keyword and definition match then the student keeps cards and has another turn. If they do not match then the student turns the cards back over and play passes to the next pupil.
- ○ Play continues until all the pairs have been identified.
- ○ The winner is the person with the most pairs.

I tend to give prizes to the winners from each group. This activity not only helps the students learn definitions but also encourages their debating skills as you often hear them discussing whether a definition is correct or not, but most importantly they tend to see it as a fun game, not learning.

EXTENSION
I sometimes ask students to produce their own cards, using their notes and textbooks to help them, as an extension to this activity.

This game can be very noisy and pupils must be given strict guidance on your expectations during such a high-spirited activity. This activity is suitable for all age groups and a variety of topics, including:

o solid, liquid or gas;
o metal or non-metal;
o plant or animal;
o male or female reproductive organs;
o conduction, convection and radiation;
o any true or false sets of questions.

BASIC IDEA

o Divide the class into two sets (I usually do boys versus girls as this tends to be the most competitive).
o Line up both groups on either side of room (ensuring both sets are the same distance from the board).
o Place two, or more, A4 cards on the board with keywords on. Number of cards depends on the subject involved, e.g. if you are asking questions on reproductive organs then one card could say 'male' and the other 'female' (again make sure cards are the same distance from each group).
o Ask a question where the answer is one of the cards on the board.
o The person at the front of each queue then runs to the board and hits (splats) the correct answer with their hand (other pupils can shout out answers).
o The winner is the first to 'splat' the correct answer (make it clear that your decision on this is final as they can be quite close together).

I keep a tally of scores on the board as we go along so the pupils can see who is winning at all times. I tend to stop when all pupils have had a go at this or time runs out.

A great activity but the pupils do get a bit excited so choose your groups for this well.

WHAT HAVE YOU LEARNT IN TODAY'S LESSON?

This is the simplest plenary activity from the teacher's point of view, but it is surprising how difficult the pupils find this. I believe this is because the question is too open and they feel they will say the wrong thing, but once they get started this works very well.

This activity is suitable for all age groups and for any subject being discussed. It also provides an excellent opportunity for you to see the true personalities of some of your students as they will 'try to be funny' and respond with non-scientific answers given half a chance, an uplifting experience for a tired teacher as well as a real reminder as to why you chose teaching as a career!

BASIC IDEA

Choose pupils to answer the question:

What have you learnt in today's lesson?

I tend to choose my weaker students first and tell them that they have the easiest task as they have everything to choose from. I continue asking this question of different students until we run out of time. If students are struggling I try to direct them a little more by asking about a specific part of the lesson.

It is interesting how attentive pupils become at this stage as they know I will 'pick on them' if they are not paying attention. It also allows you to get some communication from your quieter students as the question is 'safer' to answer.

Some fun homework activities

IDEA 59

This activity is a very simple piece of homework to set. It also makes an excellent cover lesson activity, where pupils could produce two or more of these posters.

This activity encourages pupils to think about the keywords related to a particular topic, while also providing an opportunity for the students to practise how to summarize information in a poster format. Keyword posters can be used when studying any topic and are suitable for all age ranges (the difference simply lies in the difficulty of the words involved).

BASIC IDEA

○ Pupils choose a word from a list of keywords relevant to the unit being studied (provided by you if necessary).

○ They then write this word as large a possible on an A4 piece of paper.

○ Pupils then add a single sentence definition and relevant pictures.

○ They then add colour (and their name of course).

This activity also provides you with excellent display materials for your room.

This activity not only helps students think about how essential electricity is to our modern day lives, but it also gives an opportunity for them to show off their literacy skills (or provides an opportunity for you to help improve this aspect of their work).

I use this with my Year 7 students but it is also suitable for use with other year groups whenever you are discussing electricity.

BASIC IDEA

I tell the students the following information when setting this piece of work:

- ○ the title is 'My life without electricity';
- ○ the aim is to write about what your life would be like without electricity;
- ○ you can write this as a diary entry or a descriptive essay;
- ○ you need to include some pictures;
- ○ you could imagine yourself living in an era before electricity was invented;
- ○ or could discuss what it would be like if we had a long power cut;
- ○ you could ask some of your relatives about their thoughts on this (I had one student write about 'An interview with my granddad').

Most students really enjoy this activity as it gives them a free rein and an opportunity to use their imaginations. It is also suitable for all abilities as it simply relies on them discussing their own ideas (although lower ability students may struggle to write their ideas down and asking them to do a poster showing their ideas may be more appropriate).

This activity can provide some excellent display material for your room. I find that most pupils love to have their work displayed and it can be an excellent motivation exercise.

LIFE WITHOUT ELECTRICITY

IDEA 61

MODEL CELLS

I use this activity to consolidate ideas on cell specialization after this has been introduced to my Year 7 pupils. This homework activity provides a rigorous challenge which is less academic than some of the other activities that tend to be set. It provides an opportunity for the students to show off their creative abilities and often provides some of your less academically able students with a chance to shine.

BASIC IDEA

Pupils use any materials they like to produce a model cell.

I usually tell them that the cell needs to:

- be one we have studied (including sperm cell, ciliated epithelial cell, nerve cell, red blood cell, etc.);
- show the correct structure of the cell (they are given pictures of the cells during the lesson on cell specializations);
- be appropriate colours;
- be in 3D.

As an additional motivation factor I tell the pupils that I will issue prizes for the best cells.

Several people in my department use this activity and it is interesting to see the number of 'red blood cell' cushions that appear at certain times of the year (I guess this is real magnification!).

A common homework activity in science is to ask students to write up an experiment. Although this is essential and helps build up their scientific investigation skills, the pupils can find this tedious at times. I have used this activity with several different age groups as an alternative to writing up a method, especially when the experiment involves standard techniques like testing for starch or sugar, carrying out a titration, etc.

BASIC IDEA

o Pupils carry out an experiment in the lesson (e.g. testing for starch in leaves).

o We then discuss the stages involved in this experiment and write down as bullet points.

o Homework is then to produce a worksheet explaining how to do this test.

I usually tell pupils that the worksheet needs to be:

o legible;

o easy to follow;

o in the correct order;

o include all necessary steps;

o have appropriate diagrams;

o attractive (maybe even include some colour).

As an additional motivation factor I usually tell the students that the best worksheets will be used by other groups when they do the same experiment. The pupils really like the idea of their work being used by others, possibly for years to come, and I have had some excellent worksheets produced and used by other groups.

This activity was designed to help my students remember the colours of the universal indicator pH scale.

Normally the colours for the pH scale are displayed in simple rectangles, ranging from red (pH1) through to purple (pH14). However, I found that my students were having trouble remembering these colours and believed this was due to lack of visual stimulation in a row of coloured rectangles. I therefore asked them to produce their own individual pH scale using any shape they wished with the only criteria being that the colours for each pH number must be correct.

I now tend to set this as a homework activity once the pH scale colours have been clarified. I have used this activity very successfully with Year 11 as well as Year 8 students and their recollection of the colours appears to have improved after doing this activity.

The activity involves the following:

1   draw 14 shapes (can be the same or different, but best to be related to each other);
2   label the shapes 1 to 14 (in order is best);
3   colour in part (or all) of the shape using the correct colour for the respective pH numbers;
4   add a title and your name.

A further idea would be to ask students to create their pH scale using ICT. This not only helps them learn the colours but also helps develop their computer skills.

This activity can provide you with excellent display material.

Revision techniques

This is an activity that I use mainly with my sixth form chemists but it could also be used with younger children, the main difference being that the keywords used would be simpler.

This activity not only allows pupils to check their understanding of the important scientific terms involved in a particular unit but also provides an opportunity for a competitive game (which the students love) and a chance for me to reward them with prizes, which is a great motivation factor.

RESOURCES REQUIRED
A set of cards (A8 size works well) showing the keywords from the unit being studied.

BASIC IDEA
○ Provide each student with a set of keywords on cards, with different points values for easy and harder keywords (I laminate these to make them reusable and colour code them for different point scores).
○ Allow pupils 5–10 minutes to check the definitions of their words.
○ Divide students into small groups (3s or 4s work best).
○ Students then take turns to describe their keyword to their team mates so that they can guess what is on their card.

I agree these with the students before we start. Some of their suggestions are:

○ team must guess keyword in an agreed time limit (20–30 seconds works well);
○ if 'guessing' team does not get the keyword in the allocated time then other teams can 'steal' the points – ensures whole-class involvement at all times (I ask other teams to write down their answer at this stage);
○ description *must* contain a correct scientific definition, then can use other methods of description to get team members to guess the keyword;
○ the describer cannot say any parts of the word (or words) on their card.

To enhance the students' revision further I usually ask the students to write down the keywords as they are identified and then produce revision cards as described in Idea 68, 'revision cards'.

KEYWORD GAME 2 (SIMILAR TO 'PICTIONARY')

This activity is very similar to the 'keyword game 1' (Idea 64) and again works best with smaller groups of 3s and 4s (e.g. A-level groups), although it can be done with larger classes if you get 6 to 8 students to work as two teams in competition with each other. The advantage of this is that the 'describers' are not allowed to verbally describe the word(s) and so this can be a little quieter as a larger class activity than the 'keyword game 1', although the 'guessers' tend to get a little excited/frustrated at times.

BASIC IDEA

o Provide each student with cards with keywords on, with different points values for easy and harder keywords (again I would suggest that you laminate these to make them reusable and colour code them for different point scores).

o Allow pupils 5–10 minutes to check the definitions of their words.

o Divide students into small groups (3–4 per team works best).

o Students then take turns to draw pictures related to their keyword so that their team mates can guess what is on their card – the 'describer' is only allowed to nod or shake their head in response to team's answers.

Again, a variety of rules can be imposed on this game and it is sensible to have a time limit and allow other team(s) to steal points if they can guess correctly to keep all students involved at all stages.

This is another of my favourite revision sessions that covers a couple of hours of lesson time. I have used this technique with Year 9, 10 and 11 students as they approach external examinations, although it would be suitable for other age ranges as well.

RESOURCES REQUIRED
o A5 research cards indicating the topic the students need to investigate, including several directed questions to help students find correct information (I always include a related picture to help make the cards more attractive).
o Poster materials.
o Pupils' exercise books and several textbooks.

BASIC IDEA
o Divide students into groups (size depending upon number of groups required).
o Give each group a research card.
o Pupils produce a poster advertising the topic under investigation.
o Pupils then present information to rest of class (so that all students receive a reminder of all of the necessary topics).

Alternatively, you could ask the students to present their information as a Powerpoint presentation.

POSTER PRESENTATIONS

IDEA 67

QUIZZES

An excellent revision method that I have used with all age groups, ranging from Year 7 right up to Year 13. This not only enhances the students' scientific knowledge and understanding but again introduces an opportunity to encourage their competitive spirit and give prizes as well.

There are two basic methods of doing this as highlighted below. I personally prefer the second method as it gives the students complete ownership of the quiz, but is more time consuming as will require at least two lessons.

QUIZ 1

○ Teacher writes a set of questions related to unit being revised (allows the teacher to ensure that there is a spread of easy and difficult questions).
○ Divide pupils into teams (3s or 4s work well).
○ Ask pupils to think of a team name.
○ Teacher asks questions while team records responses.

LOGISTICS

○ I find it works best if you split questions into several rounds.
○ It is useful if you mark a round before moving on to the next one so teams can see how they are progressing (I use peer marking here by simply swapping answer sheets between groups, original team then get papers back and have an opportunity to query any issues with the marking).
○ I also record their results on the board as we go – pupils enjoy seeing who is in front and how close they are to the leaders.

QUIZ 2

Works exactly as 'Quiz 1' but the students spend the initial lesson writing the questions (and correct answers) onto A7 cards. These are then handed in to the teacher who sorts them into 'rounds' ready for next lesson.

The students tend to write very easy questions but also find some very hard ones (as they hope that they will know the answer but no one else will). This encourages them to research information as well as involving them fully in a fun activity.

This method of revision is one of my favourites as it allows pupils to work at their own pace and gives them an opportunity to produce some colourful work if they wish (which helps engage both sides of their brain). This activity is suitable for all age ranges, including sixth form students.

RESOURCES REQUIRED

○ List of keywords relevant to unit being studied.
○ A7 cards in a variety of colours.
○ Colouring pens and pencils.

PRODUCING THE CARDS

1 Pupils write a keyword on front of a card.
2 Pupils use brains, notes and books to write a simple one-sentence definition on back of card.
3 Pupils repeat for all keywords on list.

USING THE CARDS

1 Sit down with cards in hands with fronts pointing upwards showing keywords.
2 Look at keyword and think of definition.
3 Check definition on back of card.
4 If definition correct one can 'discard' the card as obviously know this information (save for later use however).
5 If definition incorrect then put card on bottom of pile.
6 Continue until you can give correct definition of *all* keywords.

ADDITIONAL USES OF THE REVISION CARDS

○ Pupils can time how long it takes to get all definitions correct.
○ They could even run competitions between themselves and their friends to see who can complete the set correctly in the fastest time.
○ Students could get parents involved to help test their knowledge (as parents will have all the answers on the cards).
○ You could also use the pupils' cards for a whole-class quiz.

SUMMARIZING UNITS OF WORK

In order to help focus students' revision I believe it is important to first remind them what has been covered in the unit. There are several techniques for doing this including using bullet points or graphic organizers (spider diagrams, concept maps, etc.). The main point here, however, is to summarize the information in as few words as possible.

I find that graphic organizers are the most effective way of bringing the students' ideas together. Not only do they help students organize their thoughts and review what they already know about the subject involved but also the addition of colour allows them to use both sides of their brain to help enhance their ability to recall the required information at a later stage (i.e. during the examinations), while also producing a well presented, easily understood piece of work.

I therefore ask my students to produce a spider diagram at the end of each unit. This works very well with all year groups, although younger children need to be taught how to produce spider diagrams and I usually do the first couple of units (especially with Year 7s) together as a class, producing the spider diagram on the board as they provide me with their ideas, to help enhance their skills and then ask them to do this on their own at later stages of the year.

I then move on to use some of the other techniques discussed in this section.

I find this method particularly effective for concepts that the pupils struggle with, e.g. the Haber process and the Greenhouse Effect, as it allows you to cover any common misconceptions.

The general idea is to produce a range of statements about the concept you are revising. For example, some I have used for the Greenhouse Effect are:

o The hole in the ozone layer alters the Greenhouse Effect.
o Carbon dioxide is a greenhouse gas.
o The Greenhouse Effect is important to keep our planet warm.
o Greenhouse gases are green.
o Human activity has no effect on the Greenhouse Effect.

There are two ways in which I use these statements.

1 I produce laminated cards showing all the statements and then the pupils sort them into two piles – true or false. This is time consuming initially in terms of producing the cards but they are then reusable and ultimately save on photocopying.
2 I produce a single A4 sheet containing all the statements, which the pupils then cut out and stick onto a double page in their books. One page for true statements and the other for false statements.

In both cases I number the statements to make it easier to go over them once they have been sorted into the two sections.

I initially ask students to use their heads only to sort the statements into two sections, then after approximately 5 minutes I allow them to use books to check their responses. I then go around the room and ask students to choose a statement. They give the number of the statement (allows other students to find it easily), then read the statement aloud and indicate whether it is true or false. I then ask the class if they agree/disagree – this encourages whole-class involvement.

IDEA
71

I frequently use this idea at the end of the year with my Year 10 and Year 11 students to help prepare them for their GCSE examinations in the summer. You may, however, wish to split this up and do the relevant sections at the end of each teaching module. I find that this activity helps motivate the students as it allows them to see exactly what the exam board expects them to know.

RESOURCES REQUIRED
o A copy of the examination boards syllabus (we put these together in a booklet with a picture on the front to show the importance of this information).
o A7 cards in a variety of colours.
o Colouring pens and pencils.

FINDING OUT WHAT THEY KNOW
The first thing I ask the students to do with the syllabus statements is to read through them and identify what they know using the following:

o tick everything you are *confident* you know about;
o put a question mark next to everything you know *something* about;
o draw a cross next to everything you know *nothing* about.

The students are then asked to find out about the 'crosses' and then the 'question marks'. They are then asked to confirm what they know about the 'ticks'. You can do this by simply asking them questions or they can produce revision cards as shown below.

PRODUCING THE CARDS
1 Pupils write questions about each syllabus statement (starting with the 'crosses').
2 Pupils use brains, notes and books to write simple answers to these questions on back of each card.
3 Pupils repeat for all syllabus statements.

See 'revision cards' (Idea 68) for some suggestions as to how to use these cards.

This is an activity that I tend to use at the start of an 'end of year' revision programme for those students who will be sitting external examinations (Years 9 through to 13). It not only allows the students to check their knowledge, but it also shows them what to expect in the external examinations.

BASIC IDEA

○ Provide pupils with the previous year's examination paper.

○ Pupils complete this under examination conditions.

○ Mark papers to give pupils an idea of the grade they would have obtained.

○ Work through answers with students to deal with any misunderstandings or queries.

Some students use this as an opportunity to find out what they can do without revision. This can be very enlightening for them and usually shows a need to revise – a powerful lesson to learn at this stage!

USE OF LAST YEAR'S PAPER(S)

USE OF REVISION GUIDES

I believe that pupils of all age ranges should be encouraged to purchase revision guides to help when the time comes to revise (these are often relatively inexpensive). The big advantages of using revision guides are that they contain the bare minimum of information, so the students' brains can handle the information readily, and they are colourful and well presented, making them easier to read and understand. Some of the techniques I use to help encourage the use of the revision guides are listed below:

o pupils read a page in the revision guide, cover the information, then write down everything they can remember, check what they missed out, then retry;

o I provide the students with a list of statements related to the unit they are revising (usually taken from the national curriculum or syllabus) and then ask them to identify the page number where this information can be found in their exercise books and in the revision guides;

o I identify the pages in the revision guide related to the unit being studied, then ask pupils to use these pages to help complete a spider diagram of the unit;

o I help students produce a revision timetable on the run up to external exams, indicating which pages in the revision guide they need to learn on which evenings.

Revision guides can also be used to introduce a new topic during the initial teaching of information. I often ask pupils, of various age groups, to write bullet point notes on a particular topic using the revision guides only. We then discuss what they have learnt and add the required detail as necessary. This also enhances the students' research skills and gives them more ownership of their own learning.

Using old examination questions is one of the most effective methods of revising. Working through loads and loads of examination questions is not however the most stimulating way of revising for some students and should be used in conjunction with the other strategies discussed in this section.

I have used this strategy with Years 9 through to 13 as they approach their external examinations in the summer.

BASIC IDEA

o Provide each student with an examination question.
o Pupils complete the question individually in as much detail as possible (give an appropriate time limit depending upon marks available – I tend to give a minute per mark).
o Pupils then work in groups and add any additional comments they feel appropriate in a different colour.
o Pupils then use the mark scheme (or the teacher discusses this) to check their answer.

I then spend a few minutes discussing any queries the pupils have regarding the question. I tend to only do one or two of these at a time to reduce the boredom factor.

USE OF OLD EXAMINATION QUESTIONS

USE OF EXAMINATION QUESTIONS 2

This is another activity to help students prepare for their external examinations. It is, however, only suited to older students, who are more disciplined in their approach to independent study.

BASIC IDEA
○ Provide students with a 'question bank' (see below).
○ Ask pupils to complete over a set period of time (I tend to set this as homework over the revision period).
○ Provide pupils with answers to the 'question bank'.
○ Allow pupils time to mark and then discuss any misunderstanding or queries.

Alternatively, you can give them the questions and the answer sheets at the same time. This allows them to check their work as they go along, which can help build their confidence or at least point them in the right direction.

MAKING THE QUESTION BANKS
These are simply old examination questions that are put into sets based on the unit of the course they are examining. These are time consuming to set up initially but once they are produced they simply need photocopying for future year groups (you may wish to add questions from more current exam papers periodically).

The answer sheets are then put together from the examination mark schemes provided by the exam boards.

Students always enjoy the opportunity to use the computer systems in school. They tend not to see it as 'real' learning and will answer more questions on the computer than on a paper worksheet.

There are a huge range of CD ROMs and Internet sites available to help students revise by giving them information and testing their knowledge using simple questions (usually multiple-choice).

I have provided students of all age ranges opportunities within lessons to access computer software and the Internet to help enhance their revision programme. I tend to use this as a treat for those pupils who have worked hard throughout the whole unit and revision programme.

One of the best Internet revision sites is run by the BBC (www.bbc.co.uk/schools/revision), although there are others available. Some of these often have simple games for the students to play while also testing their scientific knowledge and understanding.

I also encourage my students to use the BBC site for revision as part of their homework.

Using ICT

In an ideal world there would always be 15 or more computers available for your class to use whenever you needed them. However, in reality, this is rarely true and frustrations can occur whenever a class teacher wishes to allow their pupils access to the computer system. However, I am a firm believer that there is always a solution to every problem.

The following suggestion is designed to relieve this frustration without abandoning the use of the computer program altogether.

RESOURCES REQUIRED

○ A single computer, desktop or laptop, that can be connected to the system you require or has the required software loaded.

○ A projector system that can be connected to your computer.

Set up the projector and computer so that your computer screen can be displayed on the whiteboard. Set up the required program and work through this with the students. This can actually sometimes be more productive than letting the students work on the program themselves as it allows you to explain any misconceptions and keep the students on task more easily.

An example of where this could be used is when carrying out the 'plotting graphs using Excel' activity (Idea 79). If I am unable to book a set of computers for this activity I set up the above system and then work through the activity step by step with the children, highlighting any misconceptions as they occur. I also have a class discussion on the best type of graph to plot, and why. We then go on to discuss appropriate titles for graphs. I then provide students with photocopies of the graph produced with some titles and axis labels etc. missing.

The students still benefit from looking at plotting graphs on Excel and also have an opportunity to discuss labelling graphs.

This is another idea to help get around the frustration of not being able to access a set of 15 computers at a time for your class. I have found that I can arrange my lessons to take advantage of the few computers in the science laboratories in my department.

RESOURCES REQUIRED

o A few computers (five is ideal, but can adapt activity to fit other numbers).
o Other independent activities lasting two lessons (or more if less computers available).

BASIC IDEA

o Introduce students to a 'circus of activities' to take place in the next three lessons – including one computer session and two lessons on other independent activitie(s).
o Divide class into three groups.
o First group works on computers, in pairs, during lesson 1, while other pupils work on other activities.
o In second lesson another group has access to the computers, while first and last group work on the other activity.
o In third lesson the last group has access to the computer.

This activity works very well during revision lessons as you can get some pupils looking at Internet revision sites on the computer while others investigate some of the ideas in the 'revision techniques' section of this book.

This activity is more suitable for use with older students due to the independent nature of the activities involved and does involve you making it very clear what you want the pupils to do. To help solve this problem, I usually provide worksheets for each activity (including the computer work) setting out what I wish the students to do for each session, otherwise I tend to be inundated with loads of questions while I 'run about' checking on the students.

STRUGGLING WITH ACCESS TO COMPUTERS FOR YOUR CLASS – SUGGESTION 2

PLOTTING GRAPHS USING EXCEL

Many students find it easier to plot graphs using the computer, especially those who struggle with their presentation. However, most pupils do not know how to plot scientific graphs correctly using this resource, simply because they have not been taught how to! The following activity has been designed to teach these graphical skills using Microsoft Excel.

Although this activity is suitable for all age groups I would suggest that these skills need to be taught early on in a child's secondary education to help them in future years.

REQUIREMENTS
- An Excel spreadsheet set up with relevant data (e.g. distance from sun, length of orbit, surface temperature, speed of orbit, mass of planet) on the computer network.
- Access to 15 computers (so pupils can work in pairs).
- 15 sets of instructions (leading pupils through the relevant steps).

BASIC IDEA
- Provide pupils with access to computers in pairs and show them how to access the required spreadsheet.
- Pupils work through worksheet, in pairs, which explains how to do the first couple of graphs, e.g. 'length of orbit against distance from sun' and 'surface temperature against distance from Sun' (alternatively you could do this as a class discussion).
- Emphasize the important points (highlight required data only [use of ctrl key], follow wizard system to plot a scatter graph, include titles, axis labels, etc.).
- Pupils then produce two other graphs following the same method (with no printed instructions).
- Pupils print graphs and add their own lines of best fit.

This activity can be extended further by providing the pupils with a range of questions related to the relationships shown by these graphs.

I would strongly suggest that you check your knowledge of Excel before proceeding with this activity as there are some real computer wizards out there!

The use of animation allows the students to visualize the scientific ideas being discussed which helps enhance their knowledge and understanding of the topic involved. These are easy to set up providing you have access to a computer and a digital projector system.

I have used this technique with a variety of age ranges and when discussing several different topics, including:

o plate tectonics;
o electrolysis;
o 3D shapes of molecules;
o fertilization of plants;
o DNA replication.

BASIC IDEA

I discuss the scientific theory behind a particular subject and then play an animation of the process involved. This allows the students to visualize the theory we have just discussed, which can be particularly useful when discussing anything to do with particles that cannot be seen very easily. I then move on to group or class discussions and questions on the topic involved.

Hint: the Internet is a good source of scientific animations.

SCIENTIFIC ANIMATIONS

IDEA

81

Computers programs provide excellent opportunities for pupils to research a variety of information. Pupils really enjoy this type of research and definitely prefer it to using books to help them.

This activity works well for a variety of topics and with all age groups. Examples of CD ROMs I have used include 'Bodyworks', 'Element & Material'.

BASIC IDEA

○ Install the required CD ROM software onto the computer system (you may need to see your computer administrator for this and make sure you have a site licence).
○ Book a set of computers for your class.
○ Produce a set of questions related to the information your students need to know, to hopefully stop them just regurgitating the information on the CD ROM.
○ Show students how to use the software.
○ Students work in pairs to use the CD ROM to find the required answers to the questions set.

I try to allow pupils to explore the information at their leisure as long as they are making progress on answering the questions. However, some pupils can get a little tied up in the amount of information available and they sometimes find it difficult to locate the required information and may need additional guidance at times. To this end I would recommend that you familiarize yourself with the workings of the particular CD ROM involved before looking at it with your class.

The best addition to my classroom over recent years is the digital projector which, when connected to a computer, allows an image of the computer screen to be displayed onto a whiteboard (or screen). This has many uses including providing the teacher with access to the Internet and software programs like Excel, etc. to use with the students. I frequently use Powerpoint (and some other software programs) to produce 'slide shows' for my students in all age ranges. This has several advantages, including:

○ clear and easily read information available for the students (can make text as large as needed);
○ providing a more stimulating visual experience for the students:
  ○ can add colour very easily;
  ○ can add fun clip-art or movie images (can also lead to some corny jokes, e.g. bonds are like bears, some are polar and others are not – I include a movie/clip-art of a polar bear which helps my A-level students remember polar bonds);
  ○ can add scientific diagrams (a scanner helps here);
  ○ can add structural formula of molecules easily (if have appropriate software).
○ provides an excellent medium for pupil presentations;
○ Powerpoint files are easily storable and available for next year's lessons at the touch of a button (remember to back up your files – I have a CD ROM for each teaching unit so it is easy for me to find the required files);
○ changing lesson objectives between lessons is very easy if slides are already prepared.

If you are lucky enough to have an interactive whiteboard you can also extend this visual experience by getting the children involved in producing diagrams or annotating web-based resources, etc. on the board, a great motivation factor for most children.

USE OF POWERPOINT AND INTERACTIVE WHITEBOARDS

Reducing the marking load

Marking pupils' work can be very time consuming and sometimes very stressful. It is, however, an essential part of a teacher's job, which helps students to progress throughout their time in school.

WRITTEN OR VERBAL FEEDBACK?

This is always a bone of contention, with some teachers trying to provide written feedback for *all* pieces of work while other, more realistic, teachers accept that this is an impossible task and in fact verbal feedback is sometimes more appropriate. See Ideas 84 to 91 for some advice on minimizing written feedback.

For the times when it is appropriate to give verbal feedback, one of the ways I have found for providing individual feedback to my students is discussed below.

BASIC IDEA

o Set an independent learning activity for the class.
o Go around the class while students are working and check pupils' work.
o Give verbal feedback on the work (you might also be able to tick work for completeness at this stage – see information below).

This is very effective as it allows you to discuss the correct approach to a piece of work with the students while also providing an opportunity for them to ask about anything they do not understand.

It is unlikely that you will be able to get round the whole class in a single lesson but you will be able to do this over several lessons.

TICKING FOR COMPLETENESS

Some pieces of work actually do not need to be checked for accuracy or correctness and simply need ticking, something I took a very long time to accept. Examples of these include when pupils have:

o made notes from the board;
o made notes from books;
o copied diagrams;
o produced poster using books, etc.

This is a technique that is commonplace in my science department for all year groups.

BASIC IDEA

In each scheme of work (lasting approximately 12 lessons) the department agrees on two pieces of work that should be marked fully with formative comments. Examples of pieces of work that are chosen tend to be focused around some of the more complex ideas in the units and include:

○ investigation write-ups;
○ literacy activities, e.g. research tasks, essay writing;
○ complex graph activities;
○ analysis of data, etc.

I then 'mark' the other pieces of work in the unit using some of the other techniques mentioned in this section so that pupils still receive a large amount of feedback on the majority of their work.

CHOOSING SPECIFIC PIECES OF WORK

CLASS MARKING

This is something I struggled with in my early years of teaching. I frequently found I did not have enough time in the class to mark the students' work. However, as the years progressed I found I was able to get through the required work at a faster rate, and I now carry out this activity frequently with all year groups.

BASIC IDEA

Pupils swap books and teacher goes over answers to the questions. Pupils then mark work either with a 'tick' or a 'cross'. More importantly, however, they must put in the correct answer if the answer given is incorrect.

I tend to ask pupils to give me the answers as this allows more pupil involvement in these sessions. It also provides an opportunity to get some of your quieter students involved as they feel 'safer' answering questions when they have already had time to think about the answer.

I also ask them to give a total mark and ask for hands up for who got 10 out of 10, 9 out of 10, etc. (pupils, especially the younger ones, love to share their successes and this provides an excellent opportunity for this).

TYPES OF ACTIVITIES

Not all activities are suitable for whole-class marking but examples include:

o single-word answer questions;
o fill in the gap exercises;
o calculations.

Learning to use this technique had a profound effect on lowering my marking load, while still providing the students with feedback on their work. In fact, it provides the students with instant feedback which is often more effective. It also allows you to deal with any misconceptions as they are highlighted during the marking process.

It is always interesting to see that no matter what you tell the students at the start of an activity, common errors are frequently seen in certain pieces of work. It is not sensible in these situations to write the same thing 30 times (or even more, if you teach more that one set in a particular year group).

One of the easiest strategies for dealing with this is to give the pupils verbal feedback related to the issue involved. You could also ask the students to write down this feedback if you feel it is important to have this recorded to help them in future.

See the next few pages for other ideas.

DEALING WITH COMMON ERRORS – VERBAL FEEDBACK

IDEA
87

This is my favourite way of dealing with common errors in pupils' work. I have used it with all year groups (including my A-level students).

BASIC IDEA

Whenever I mark specific pieces of work it soon becomes obvious if common errors are occurring. If this is the case, I produce some stickers stating the comment I would write in response to this error. I usually try and add an appropriate 'clip-art' as well to make the stickers more attractive. I then simply place the stickers onto the pupils' work, resulting in less writing for me.

Producing the stickers initially can be time consuming but you tend to find you can reuse them in later years.

Examples of a couple of these stickers are shown below.

> **Title missing or incomplete** – retry please.
> _____
> A graph to show . . . is a good starting point.

> Remember to use a ruler for **all** straight lines.

This works very well when marking investigation write-ups and can be used with all year groups.

BASIC IDEA

○ Produce a table with three columns.
○ In first column write general points that tend to be 'missing' from the pupils work (as many or few as you feel are necessary).
○ Label second column 'attempted'.
○ Label third column 'completed'.
○ Include a description of the table (see example below).
○ Stick into pupil's book and tick appropriate columns depending upon whether information included, or not.
○ Ask pupils to complete.

Year 9 – metals and acid investigation

The table below shows the information that should have been included in your conclusion for this experiment. Two ticks means you have completed the section indicated, well done. However, crosses mean you still have work to do on these sections and these must be completed by the date shown below. Look carefully at the comments I have written on your work.

Date to be completed by _____

Description	Attempted	Completed (well done)
Graph		
Relationship between variables		
Reactivity of each experiment		
Graph used to discuss reactivity		
Scientific reason given explaining different rates of reactions		
Accuracy of prediction discussed		

DEALING WITH COMMON ERRORS – TABLES

IDEA

89

This is an activity that I use mainly with my A-level students as I feel they have the maturity to benefit from this rather than just using the mark scheme to 'cheat'. I do however usually ask to see their work before handing out the mark scheme to ensure they have at least attempted all of the questions required.

BASIC IDEA

○ Ask students to complete a set of questions on the topic being studied.

○ Check students have completed all questions.

○ Provide them with the answer sheet and ask them to mark their own work, remembering to add the correct answer if they do not get it correct (it works best if they mark in a different colour to allow them to see where they struggled when revising later).

This activity also helps students develop independent learning skills and gives them more ownership of their own learning.

MAKING USE OF MARK SCHEMES

Sometimes, even in science, it is necessary to set essay-type questions. This not only allows the students to group together relevant information in an appropriate format but it also provides them with an opportunity to 'show off' their literacy skills, or it allows you to help them improve this aspect of their learning.

I often find that students do not include the necessary information in their essays, even if they are given a writing frame to help them. Marking their work can be very time consuming as you find yourself writing out 'you need to include ...' several times. I have therefore designed tables to help with this type of marking.

BASIC IDEA

o Produce a table as shown in the example below.
o Stick into pupils' books.
o Add tick or crosses as appropriate, depending upon whether information is included or not.
o Ask pupils to complete essay.

The following table shows the information that should have been included in your Noble gases essay. A tick means you have included the information, well done. A cross however means you need to add this information to your essay.

Other names for this group	
Use of helium	
Use of argon	
Use of neon	
Use of krypton	
Number of electrons in outer shell	
Why do they not react very easily?	
Non-metal or metal?	
State of matter at room temperature	
Monoatomic? (explain what this means)	

IDEA
91

MARKING ESSAYS – PEER MARKING

This activity works well with older pupils, especially A-level students. I find this activity very effective when marking 'essay-type' examination questions. It not only reduces the teacher's marking load, but it also gives the students, as markers, an insight into the way their work will be marked by the examiners in the external exams. This hopefully helps to improve their responses to these questions and consequently helps improve their overall grades at the end of the year.

BASIC IDEA

- After pupils have completed an essay-type question, collect the scripts and redistribute to different students (it is sometimes possible to swap scripts between different teaching groups).
- Provide pupils with the examination mark scheme for the essay.
- Pupils then use mark scheme to mark scripts and give the essay a mark.

I often provide a separate sheet for pupils to record the marks on and usually ask the students to mark two scripts each and then mark their own work. This not only gives them a better idea of their mark but also allows them to get to grips with the mark scheme, as they are sometimes difficult to understand.

When the students mark their own script I ask them to annotate the scripts to shown where they believe they achieved specific marks (the mark schemes tend to have codes for particular points) which allows me to scan mark them if all three results are very different.

Science in the outside world

The newspapers, and Internet news sites, are full of interesting scientific facts and some spectacular pictures, including natural phenomenon, e.g. coral reefs, as well as natural disasters like the Tsunami disaster on Boxing Day 2004. Whenever these reports appear in the paper I tend to buy several copies and mount the information on cards and laminate them for use by my students (or you could print the information off the Internet).

A couple of ways I use this information are shown below:

○ **Display material**: recent materials are displayed at the entrance to my classroom so that pupils can read them as they are waiting to enter the room;
○ **Research projects**: the newspaper articles make an excellent starting point for any relevant research project. These research projects may fit into a unit of work, e.g. the Tsunami disaster of 2004 works well when discussing plate tectonics theory. Or they could be set as individual projects at the end of the year.

Using newspaper reports allows you to provide scientific information to your students, while also drawing their attention to what is going on in the world around us. It is, however, important to keep your newspaper articles as recent as possible so that the students see them as relevant, rather than old news.

There is nothing like a school trip to get pupils excited and teachers stressed, but it really is worthwhile. Some of the trips that I have been involved in include:

○ **Zoo trip**: simply the best science trip in my opinion. The pupils love looking at the animals and if you provide them with worksheets they can also learn lots about adaptations;

○ **Science museum trip**: another excellent opportunity for students to learn a large amount of science. Again, providing a worksheet can focus their learning. Some museums even do 'sleepovers' – a truly different experience;

○ **Lectures**: universities and some companies host science lectures which can be very entertaining. Our Year 11s and 12s recently attended a lecture of 'Fantastic Plastics' which left them talking about plastics all the way home;

○ **University visits**: some universities are more than willing to run laboratory sessions to help your students decide whether to continue with sciences into sixth form and beyond.

School trips are a great motivation factor for the children but can involve a large amount of paperwork for the teacher. It is important that you double check your transport bookings to avoid disappointment – however, be prepared and everything will go well and the children will be appreciative, honestly!

Maintaining the WOW factor

DISAPPEARING POLYSTYRENE

This is an excellent demonstration which really gets the students thinking and in awe of science. I use this with my Year 11 students to demonstrate some of the properties of plastics, but it can also be used as a starting point for discussions into the recycling of plastics. I usually do this demonstration at the end of the lesson and ask the students to provide an explanation by the next lesson.

REQUIRED RESOURCES
o Large beaker (1 litre).
o Propanone.
o Expanded polystyrene chips.
o Expanded polystyrene cups.

INSTRUCTIONS
o Place approximately 100 cm³ of propanone in the beaker.
o Add polystyrene chips and watch them fizz and reduce in size dramatically (I often give each pupil a polystyrene chip to add).
o Then add a polystyrene cup and watch it 'disappear' (a bit like the Wicked Witch of the West melting in *The Wizard of Oz*).
o Pupils will ask to see this over and over again – especially the cups.
o Decant off acetone to show pupils 'slimy' polystyrene (can leave to harden and show them this in the next lesson as well).

THEORY
Expanded polystyrene (EPS) is produced by a complex process involving a blowing agent and polystyrene granules, which eventually results in air being incorporated in the expanded polystyrene to give the classic foam we use as insulating material.

The polystyrene does not actually 'disappear' into the propanone. The propanone softens the plastic (allowing the polymer chains to separate) and the air is released (hence the fizzing observed) and the volume now occupied by the polystyrene is dramatically reduced.

Students love this demonstration as it produces huge flames (and a huge bang if you try the extension part). I use this with my Year 10 students to demonstrate combustion reactions, although it is also perfect for open evening where it attracts a large amount of interest and a few wobbly legs!

REQUIREMENTS
o Washing-up bowl full of soapy water (produced using washing-up liquid).
o Methane supply (a long rubber tube attached to a gas tap works well for this).
o Oxygen supply (an oxygen cylinder with a long rubber tube attached is best).
o Bunsen burner.
o Safety screens.
o Goggles for the students.
o A steady hand and a healthy heart.

INSTRUCTIONS
Make sure the apparatus is surrounded by safety screens. I would also strongly recommend that you try this first before demonstrating it to the students as it is pretty reactive.

1 Bubble some methane gas into the soapy water in the washing-up bowl.
2 Light a splint from a Bunsen burner (which is placed well away from the washing-up bowl).
3 'Throw' the splint into the washing-up bowl and **stand well back**.

Large flames (nearly to the ceiling) will be observed, usually resulting in the students taking a large step backwards and exclaiming 'wow Miss!'.

EXTENSION
Bubble oxygen gas as well as methane gas in to the water in the washing-up bowl. Then repeat the instructions as above. This will result in large flames (which observers now expect) but will also cause a huge bang (unexpected, resulting in a few wobbly legs – usually from parents at open evening).

This demonstration is one of the best I have ever seen. The students love it and want to watch it over and over again. I use this with my Year 10 students to demonstrate a highly exothermic reaction, although it can also be used to demonstrate oxidation reactions. This demonstration is perfect for open evenings where it attracts a large amount of interest.

REQUIRED RESOURCES
o Jelly babies (make sure they fit easily into the boiling tubes).
o Potassium chlorate.
o Spatula.
o Boiling tubes and holder.
o Bunsen burner and heatproof mat.
o Tongs.
o Test-tube rack.
o Safety screens.
o Goggles for students.
o Full face visor for you.

INSTRUCTIONS
Make sure the apparatus is surrounded by safety screens. I would also strongly recommend that you try this first before demonstrating it to the students as it is pretty reactive.

1 Place two spatulas of potassium chlorate into a boiling tube.
2 Heat the tube carefully until the potassium chlorate melts.
3 Place the boiling tube carefully into the test-tube rack.
4 Using the tongs add a jelly baby to the melted potassium chlorate and **stand well back**.

As the jelly baby reacts with the potassium chlorate a large amount of smoke, as well as heat and flames, and a very sweet (candyfloss type) smell is released so it is probably best to do this at the end of a day.

The potassium chlorate is a very strong oxidizing agent which rapidly oxidizes the sugar in the jelly baby resulting in the highly exothermic reaction observed.

If you use a wooden test-tube rack you will be able to show how hot the experiment was as it will have charred the wood leaving a lovely black mark.

This demonstration is designed to maintain the students' interest in science, as well as encouraging their natural curiosity and scientific thinking. We use this with our Year 7s at the end of their first secondary school science lesson, asking them to return next lesson with an explanation of how it works. This keeps them talking about the science after the bell has gone!

REQUIREMENTS
- Photocopies of a £5 note × 3.
- Container of water.
- Container of ethanol and a pinch of salt (adds colour to the flame so students can see flame clearly).
- Container of water, ethanol and a pinch of salt.
- Bunsen burner.
- Tongs.
- Heatproof mat × 2.

INSTRUCTIONS
At the start of the lesson soak each of the £5 notes in a different solution (do not let the students know what is in each container).

'Burn' each of the £5 notes by holding them over a blue flame using a pair of tongs, each time asking the students to predict what they think will happen (you may even want to extend their thinking and ask 'why?').

The notes should be burnt in the following order:

1 £5 note in ethanol (will burn rapidly as ethanol is highly flammable and will quickly turn to ash – can leave to finish burning on second heatproof mat);
2 £5 note in water (will not burn very easily as water prevents oxygen reaching the paper and therefore stops it burning – but be careful if it dries out as it will burn as normal);
3 £5 note in water and ethanol (the ethanol will burn violently but the £5 note will not burn as it is wet).

At the end of the demonstration ask students to come up with an explanation of these three experiments by next lesson. This provides an excellent starter activity for your next lesson.

This can be carried out as a demonstration or a class practical. I use this to demonstrate to Year 8 students the reactions of acid and alkali, but it is also very effective as a 'science club' activity.

RESOURCES REQUIRED
○ Small conical flask (100 cm³).
○ Ethanoic acid.
○ Sodium bicarbonate.
○ Food colouring.
○ Large tray.
○ Spatula.
○ Measuring cylinder.

INSTRUCTIONS
○ Place 2–3 spatulas of sodium bicarbonate in the conical flask.
○ Place flask in centre of tray.
○ Measure out 50 cm³ of ethanoic acid into the measuring cylinder.
○ Add food colouring to the acid.
○ Pour the acid into the flask, quickly, and watch the volcano erupt.

Alternatively you can add universal indicator to the acid, instead of food colouring, to see some colour changes as the volcano erupts.

If you wished to extend this into a longer activity then you could get the pupils to produce a model volcano, around the conical flask, before adding the chemicals. Paper maché and poster paints work well for this.

EXPLODING VOLCANO 1

EXPLODING VOLCANO 2

This is another excellent visual demonstration. I have previously used this when introducing the rock cycle to Year 8s but it is also an excellent demonstration to show to Year 7s at the start of their secondary science course. This demonstration can also be used to illustrate oxidation reactions, as well as reactions of transition metals for A-level chemists.

RESOURCES REQUIRED
- Large conical flask (1 litre).
- Ammonium dichromate(VI) (approximately 10 g).
- Glass wool.
- Bunsen burner.
- Heatproof mat.
- Tripod and gauze.

INSTRUCTIONS
- Place the ammonium dichromate(VI) into the conical flask.
- Place a loose plug of glass wool in the mouth of the flask (to prevent the escape of chromium oxide produced).
- Stand the conical flask on a tripod and gauze, then heat strongly from below with a roaring Bunsen flame.

Alternatively, you can also do this without the conical flask by simply placing the dichromate in a conical pile on a heatproof mat (*must* be done in a fume hood).

You can also start the reaction using a 3 cm wooden splint soaked in ethanol and stick this into the pile of ammonium dichromate to act as a wick, rather than using a Bunsen burner.

As the orange ammonium dichromate(VI) is heated (by the Bunsen burner or via the lit splint), it decomposes to produce green chromium(III) oxide (which has a considerably greater volume that the ammonium dichromate). This decomposition is accompanied by several sparks (as well as the dramatic colour change) and some of the oxide will shoot upwards from the 'volcano'. The volcano can last for up to a minute.

The reaction that occurs is:

$$(NH_4)_2Cr_2O_{7\ (s)} \rightarrow Cr_2O_{3\ (s)} + N_{2\ (g)} + 4H_2O_{\ (l)}$$

BLUSHING FLOWERS

This demonstration is another one of those phenomenon that really gets the student thinking and discussing how things work. I have used this activity when introducing pupils to indicators and have found it suitable for all age ranges.

REQUIRED RESOURCES
○ Several white flowers (carnations work well).
○ Phenolphthalein indicator.
○ A vase (or a glass beaker).
○ Small beaker.
○ Plant sprayer containing 0.1 mol dm^{-3} sodium carbonate solution (should have a pH > 11 for an instant reaction).

INSTRUCTIONS
Before the lesson soak one of the carnations in the phenolphthalein solution. Allow the flower to dry, then place it in the vase with the other flowers. Place the vase of flowers in a prominent position ready for the lesson.

While I start discussing indicators I start 'talking sweetly' to the flowers and spray them with the solution in the plant sprayer, and watch one of the flowers 'blush' as it turns a magenta pink colour. This causes much hilarity as pupils think the flower is embarrassed.

I then go on to discuss why the flower 'blushed' and why we need indicators. This is also an excellent lead into making students aware of the range of indicators available.

It is sometimes possible to return the flower to its original colour by spraying with colourless vinegar (or other dilute acid).

SAFETY
Be careful when using the spray – make sure everyone is wearing eye protection and empty the sprayer as soon as possible.